WOOLF'S *TO THE LIGHTHOUSE*

Continuum Reader's Guides

Continuum Reader's Guides are clear, concise and accessible introductions to classic literary texts. Each book explores the themes, context, criticism and influence of key works, providing a practical introduction to close reading and guiding the reader towards a thorough understanding of the text. Ideal for undergraduate students, the guides provide an essential resource for anyone who needs to get to grips with a literary text.

Achebe's *Things Fall Apart* – Ode Ogede
Austen's *Emma* – Gregg A. Hecimovich
Bram Stoker's *Dracula* – William Hughes
Chaucer's *The Canterbury Tales* – Gail Ashton
Conrad's *Heart of Darkness* – Allan Simmons
Dickens's *Great Expectations* – Ian Brinton
Eliot's *Middlemarch* – Josie Billington
Fitzgerald's *The Great Gatsby* – Nicolas Tredell
Fowles's *The French Lieutenant's Woman* – William Stephenson
James's *The Turn of the Screw* – Leonard Orr
Joyce's *Ulysses* – Sean Sheehan
Salinger's *The Catcher in the Rye* – Sarah Graham
William Blake's Poetry – Jonathan Roberts

WOOLF'S *TO THE LIGHTHOUSE*

A READER'S GUIDE

JANET WINSTON

continuum

Continuum International Publishing Group

The Tower Building
11 York Road
London SE1 7NX

80 Maiden Lane
Suite 704, New York
NY 10038

www.continuumbooks.com

British Library Cataloguing-in-Publication Data
A catalogue record for this book is available from the
British Library.

ISBN: 978-0-8264-9582-2 (hardback)
          978-0-8264-9583-9 (paperback)

Library of Congress Cataloging-in-Publication Data
Winston, Janet.
Woolf's To the lighthouse: a reader's guide/Janet Winston.
p. cm.
Includes bibliographical references and index.
ISBN 978-0-8264-9582-2 – ISBN 978-0-8264-9583-9 (pbk.)
1. Woolf, Virginia, 1882-1941. To the lighthouse. I. Title.
PR6045.O72T6875 2009
823'.912–dc22   2009010918

Typeset by Newgen Imaging Systems Pvt Ltd, Chennai, India
Printed and bound in Great Britain by the MPG Books Group

For my parents, Seymour and Trudi Winston

and

in memory of Rose Giannini

CONTENTS

ACKNOWLEDGMENTS

I would like to thank The Society of Authors as the Literary Representative of the Estate of Virginia Woolf for permission to quote from Woolf's work. I also thank The Henry W. and Albert A. Berg Collection of English and American Literature, The New York Public Library, Astor, Lenox and Tilden Foundations for permission to quote from Woolf's manuscripts; the Virginia Woolf Estate and The Random House Group Limited for permission to reproduce passages from *The Diaries of Virginia Woolf*, *The Letters of Virginia Woolf*, *The Essays of Virginia Woolf*, and *Moments of Being* published by Hogarth Press; and the Houghton Mifflin Harcourt Publishing Company for permission to use excerpts from *The Common Reader*, *The Diaries of Virginia Woolf*, *The Essays of Virginia Woolf*, *Moments of Being*, *A Passionate Apprentice: The Early Journals of Virginia Woolf*, *A Room of One's Own*, *Three Guineas*, and *To the Lighthouse*. My thanks go to Adele Edling Shank for permission to quote from the published playscript of her 2007 theatrical adaptation of *To the Lighthouse*. I am grateful to her and to Suzanne Bellamy and Marilyn Andrews for their generosity in discussing their art with me. Thanks also go to Lisa Dowdeswell for The Society of Authors, Gabrielle White for Random House, Ralph Marquez for Houghton Mifflin Harcourt, and Isaac Gewirtz, Curator of the Berg Collection, for their expeditious assistance with securing copyright permissions.

I gratefully acknowledge Continuum Books, especially my editor Anna Fleming for commissioning me to write this book and patiently working with me throughout the process. My thanks also go to Colleen Coalter for her always prompt and liberal assistance; and to

Mr. P. Muralidharan for his efficacious command of the copyediting process.

I am tremendously appreciative of the incisive comments and suggestions offered by Jeanette McVicker and Suzanne Raitt on an earlier version of the manuscript. A debt of gratitude goes to Denise Nico Leto for lending her unfailing critical eye to the manuscript as well as freely giving advice in times of crisis. I could not have imagined a smarter, more scrupulous research assistant than Matthew Franks, and for that I am thankful. All of their efforts on my behalf have helped make this a better book.

My colleagues in the English Department at Humboldt State University deserve recognition for their congeniality, intelligence, and support. I am especially indebted to Christina Accomando, who generously mentored me throughout the process of seeing this first book into publication. Warm thanks also go to Terry Santos for her camaraderie and unflagging support. I greatly appreciate Susan Bennett for granting me an additional course reduction in spring 2007 and a research budget, and Michael Eldridge for helping with hiring negotiations and my transition to HSU. I would like to acknowledge Kenneth Ayoob for his generous financial support and Humboldt State University's Sponsored Programs Foundation for awarding me a small grant. I extend my thanks as well to my Richmond, Virginia colleagues Laura Browder, L. Carol Summers, Sydney Watts, and Abigail Cheever for their sage advice and helpful feedback on my book proposal.

I wish to acknowledge the students in my Woolf courses over the years, "Virginia Woolf and Her Legacy in Contemporary Literature and Culture" (Spring 2005), "Virginia Woolf and the Bloomsbury Group Revisited" (Spring 2005), "Art and Politics in Virginia Woolf and the Bloomsbury Group" (Spring 2007), and "Art, War, and Politics in Modernist Literature" (Spring 2009). They motivated me with their intelligence and passion to make Woolf accessible to a larger circle of "common readers."

I have been inspired by the work of Woolf colleagues from around the world, too numerous to name. My deepest appreciation goes to Eileen Barrett and Mary Lou Emery, who fostered in me the love of reading *To the Lighthouse*, and to G. Jennifer Wilson for teaching me how one should read a book. I also wish to thank Jane Lilienfeld, Mark Hussey, Leslie Hankins, and Vara Neverow, who have both inspired and encouraged me along the way.

ACKNOWLEDGMENTS

A debt of gratitude is due my friends and family for their love and unwavering support throughout the book-writing process, especially Trudi and Seymour Winston, Carol Winston, Roseanne Quinn, Rose Quinn, Patricia Perry, Laura Miller, Steve Miller, David Miller, Alyssa Miller, and María Corral-Ribordy. I want to thank especially Mary Jane Smith, whose fierce intelligence, integrity, and eagerness to engage in endless conversations about Virginia Woolf—despite her reluctance to embrace Woolf ever since reading *Orlando*—emboldened me to complete this book.

CHAPTER 1

CONTEXTS

[W]e can watch the famous dead in their familiar habits and fancy sometimes that we are very close and can surprise their secrets. [. . .] How far, we must ask ourselves, is a book influenced by its writer's life [. . .]?
—Virginia Woolf, "How Should One Read a Book?," 1932, Essays 5

I received the copies of the Modern edition of To The Lighthouse safely. I could wish [. . .] that the introducer did not think it necessary to drag in my private life.
—Virginia Woolf, Letter to Donald Brace of Harcourt, Brace, & Co., 1937, Letters 6

Despite Virginia Woolf's wish to keep her private life separate from her published writing, information about her upbringing, education, friends and lovers—the focus of this chapter—contributes greatly to one's understanding of her creative work, especially *To the Lighthouse*, her most autobiographical novel.

THE VICTORIAN FAMILY

Virginia Woolf was born in 1882 into an upper-middle-class Victorian family. The men on both sides of her extended family attended elite educational institutions (Eton and Cambridge University) and became professionals in such fields as colonial administration in India, law, medicine, and writing. Woolf's parents, who were themselves writers, had family ties to noted literary figures and visual artists of their day. For example, Woolf's father, Leslie Stephen, initially married Harriet

Marian ("Minny") Thackeray, the youngest daughter of nineteenth-century novelist William Makepeace Thackeray. Minny's premature death in 1875, after eight years of marriage, precipitated Leslie's marrying her friend Julia Prinsep [née Jackson], Woolf's mother, in 1878. Julia's first husband, Herbert Duckworth, whom she had married in 1867, had died prematurely in 1870, leaving her with three children: George, Stella, and Gerald.

Julia, who as a child had spent years in the care of her maternal aunt's family, Thoby and Sara Prinsep and their four children, grew up in close proximity to many of Victorian England's artistic elite. Such figures as Alfred Tennyson, John Ruskin, and the pre-Raphaelite painter John Everett Millais frequented her aunt Sara's salons (Hussey, *Virginia Woolf A to Z* 218). Famed photographer Julia Margaret Cameron was another of her maternal aunts. Aunt Sara's son Valentine ("Val") Cameron Prinsep would become a prominent portrait and historical painter.

During Julia's marriage to Leslie Stephen, writing remained a sideline rather than a full-time occupation. She managed the Stephen household, which included domestic servants and, with the birth of two more daughters (Vanessa and Virginia) and two more sons (Thoby and Adrian), eventually eight children from their blended families, including her stepchild, Laura, who was developmentally disabled (Lee 99–103). In addition to the immediate domestic responsibilities, such as educating her children, Julia Stephen served as a self-taught, unpaid caregiver for her extended family and, during the summer months when the Stephen family vacationed in Cornwall, for the sick of the St. Ives fishing community (Lee 26, 97–98). She wrote about the vocation of nursing in *Notes from Sick Rooms* (1883), the only essay of hers published during her lifetime (Zwerdling 188–90). She also wrote children's stories, which, along with her essays, were finally published in 1987.

Woolf's father, Leslie Stephen, was a man of letters—a professional essayist, editor, and literary critic, who counted the novelists and poets Thomas Hardy, Henry James, and James Russell Lowell among his friends. Educated at Cambridge University in religion and ordained as an Anglican parson, he instead pursued, after a brief stint as a Cambridge tutor, a career as an independent scholarly writer. He tackled a range of subjects, from ethics, utilitarianism, and agnosticism to eighteenth-century literature and thought to Alpine climbing, a favorite past-time. Today he is best remembered for editing the first twenty-six volumes of the massive *Dictionary of National Biography*. His appointment to the Presidency of the London Library in 1892 and his knighthood in 1902 indicate his repute as a late-Victorian intellectual (Hussey, *Virginia Woolf A to Z* 270–71; Lee 68–73, 98–99).

Woolf's fondest memories of her parents were from childhood during family holidays in St. Ives (Briggs, *Virginia Woolf* 162–63). Located in Cornwall, on England's rugged southwest coast, this pilchard fishing village contained Talland House, on which Leslie Stephen had taken out a long-term lease. Every summer, he packed up his London home at 22 Hyde Park Gate and moved his family and servants for two months from the metropolitan center of England to its far southwestern tip. In St. Ives the children looked for shells and played cricket. Leslie Stephen would hire a fishing boat and take them on the bay. The children spotted porpoises and sailed to Godrevy Lighthouse (V. Woolf and V. Bell 91, 94, 108, 118). Upon returning years later, Woolf referred to Godrevy as "my Lighthouse" (*Letters* 4: 165) and to the landscape surrounding St. Ives as "our mistress" (*Passionate* 283). For Woolf, the sea at St. Ives was "a miracle—more congenial to me than any human being" (*Letters* 1: 326).

In her memoir "A Sketch of the Past," Woolf identifies her first and most important memories from childhood: in one, she is sitting on her mother's lap, surrounded by the red and purple flowers of her mother's print dress, on the trip home from St. Ives; in another, while in a semi-conscious state just before waking in the Talland House nursery, she is listening to waves crashing on the shore and the nursery blind flapping in the breeze. "If life has a base that it stands upon, if it is a bowl that one fills and fills and fills—then my bowl without a doubt stands upon this memory" ("Sketch" 64). This all-important second memory leads Woolf to recall seeing her mother, dressed in a white nightgown, standing on her parents' bedroom balcony, surrounded by vines of purple and silver passion flowers ("Sketch" 65-66).

When Julia Stephen died suddenly in 1895, her youngest daughter was thirteen, and the joyous family hub Julia had created dissolved (V. Woolf, "Sketch" 81–84); it was replaced with her father's domineering presence, which now overshadowed everything. For decades, Woolf was haunted by her mother. She eventually wrote *To the Lighthouse* to lay the memory of her mother and Leslie Stephen to rest (V. Woolf, *Diary* 3: 208; "Sketch" 81; *Letters* 3: 374).

Her diary contains an outline of her initial ideas for the book: "father & mother & child in the garden: the death; the sail to the lighthouse. [. . .] It might contain all characters boiled down; & childhood; & then this impersonal thing, [. . .] the flight of time [. . .]" (3: 36).

The facts about Woolf's parentage suggest three underlying themes prevalent within her Victorian upbringing: distinct sex roles, service to family, nation, and empire, and intellectualism. The first two themes accurately characterize most Victorian families of Woolf's race and class. In keeping with the legal and economic barriers and social mores of the time, the majority of women of Woolf's class married, bore children, and managed the household as their primary life's work. In contrast to their male siblings, they were educated at home through a combination of home-schooling, governesses, and tutors. As was the case with Virginia Stephen, many young women were additionally sent to finishing schools to learn proper social etiquette and deportment necessary to develop appropriately refined feminine behavior (V. Woolf and V. Bell 152). Throughout her oeuvre and especially in *A Room of One's Own*, Woolf denounces the inequitable educational opportunities afforded Englishwomen of her class. Though she educated herself by reading vociferously the volumes contained within her father's personal library and attended Greek and Latin classes at King's College, London, she remained resentful about being denied the Cambridge University education that Victorian men, such as her brothers and male friends, received (for a discussion of Woolf's education in philosophy, see Banfield, *Phantom* 26–30). In a passage from one of her letters written to her friend Desmond MacCarthy one month before her death, Woolf sums up her lifelong feelings on the matter: "Compare my wretched little £150 education with yours, with Lytton's [Strachey], with Leonard's [Woolf]. Did Eton and Cambridge make no difference to you? [. . .] Would Lytton have written just as well if he'd spent his youth, as I did mine, mooning among books in a library? [. . .] If you knew my inadequacy; what shifts and squeaks I'm put to every time I dip my pen!" (6: 467–68).

With equal intensity, Woolf rails in her writings against the suffocating effects the institution of the middle-class Victorian family could have on a woman's life, including her own. Typically headed by a male figure or figures—in Woolf's case this included her father as well as her two stepbrothers—the family reproduced itself by reinforcing women's dependency on men as virtual chattel in the marriage market. In "A Sketch of the Past" Woolf fleshes out middle-class women's conventional place in Victorian society and the debasing rituals of domestic life that exerted pressure to establish them there: "Hyde Park Gate in 1900 was a complete model of Victorian society. [. . .] Society in those days was a perfectly competent, perfectly complacent, ruthless machine. A girl had no chance against its fangs. No other desires [than marriage]—say to paint, or to write—could be taken seriously" (147, 157). Afternoons required dressing for tea and making polite conversation with her father and guests; however, evenings were when "[s]ociety exerted its full pressure" ("Sketch" 155). Before attending a party or the opera arranged by her status-conscious stepbrother George, she would have to dress again and submit to George's "extraordinarily observant scrutiny," "as if [she] [. . .] were a horse brought into the show ring" ("Sketch" 151). The nineteenth-century feminine ideal, as Woolf describes it here or as it was enshrined in Coventry Patmore's poem *The Angel in the House*, offered little sustenance for intellectually- and artistically-minded, iconoclastic women. Woolf's feelings for her father defy one-dimensional descriptions (Lee 68–71, 724). As the model for Mr. Ramsay, the Victorian patriarch in *To the Lighthouse*, Leslie Stephen appears in his daughter's writings as both dictatorial brute and soft-spoken contemplator. For example, in "A Sketch of the Past" she describes his bullying behavior toward his daughters after Julia Stephen's death in 1895 as that of "a typical [male] Victorian" (147) for whom "woman was then (though gilt with an angelic surface) the slave" (145). Yet, she concedes, in contrast to her stepbrothers, he modeled the life of the mind and encouraged her literary acumen: "No one cared less for the conventions. [. . .] Nobody respected intellect more. [. . .] Slowly he would unwrinkle his forehead and come to ground and realise with a very sweet smile that I stood there [in his study]. Rising he would go to the shelves, put the book back, and ask me gently, kindly; 'What did you make of it?'" ("Sketch" 157). Twenty-four years after Leslie Stephen's death in 1904, on the ninety-sixth anniversary of his birth, Woolf remarked in her diary that had he lived on (she was twenty-two years old when he died), "[h]is life would have entirely ended mine. What would have happened? No writing, no books;—inconceivable" (3: 208).

Just as Woolf's feelings for her father are incongruous, so too is her critique of elitism. Much has been written about Woolf's class snobbery; more recently, critics have begun to address her attitudes about blacks and Jews. Disconcerting as it may be for some readers, Woolf's incisive critiques of patriarchal institutions and male misogyny exist alongside expressions of well-developed feelings of superiority—and disgust for others whose appearances and behaviors fall outside her norms. In one of several vitriolic descriptions of her mother-in-law, Marie Woolf—comments inflamed by Woolf's anti-Semitism and snobbish disgust for lower-middle-class tastes and conventions—she remarks in her diary on Mrs. Woolf's penchant to express herself in cloying cant:

> so vampire like & vast in her demand for my entire attention & sympathy, [. . .] talking about [. . .] the niceness of everybody, & how she will come to Worthing every year, & will expect to come to tea with us. Lord Lord! how many daughters have been murdered by women like this! What a net of falsity they spread over life. (3: 321)

These remarks appear to reflect Woolf's serious social critique of the role women play in the family to constrain their daughters. Mothers who uphold middle-class family values of conventionality in manners and taste, materialism, and rigid gender roles, as in expecting women to play hostess and listen sympathetically on command, bequeath a legacy of shallowness and suffering to their daughters.

The credibility of Woolf's argument is undercut, however, by its framing, which indicts the entire Woolf clan:

> [. . .] I begin to see very plainly how ugly, how nosey, how irreparably middle class they all are. Indeed, my aesthetic sense is the one that protests most obstinately—how they cheapen the house & garden—How they bring in an atmosphere of Earls Court & hotels, how impossibly out of place, & stuffy & towny & dressy & dowdy they look on the terrace, among apple trees & vegetables & flowers! (*Diary* 3: 320–21)

Here, as in Woolf's descriptions of Mrs. Woolf's "dreary furs & ugly bonnet & large boots, with her pendulous cheeks & red nose & cheap earrings" (*Diary* 3: 321), Woolf's critique of women's familial roles all but collapses under the weight of her expression of disgust for her in-laws. Through the senses of sight and (aesthetic) taste, Woolf registers her revulsion in terms laden with markers of class and race. Through Woolf's eyes, the bodies of her lower-middle-class Jewish family appear monstrous and defile the beauty of nature seen from the terrace.

Merciless critiques of family and friends were commonplace for Woolf. Many of these sketches, scattered throughout Woolf's letters and diaries, were aimed to entertain (Nicolson, "Bloomsbury" 11–13). Others strike one as cathartic invective. Several reveal undeniably racist, classist, and anti-Semitic sentiments, as in Woolf's 1930 letter to the composer Ethel Smyth in which Woolf recalls her abhorrence of marrying a Jew (Leonard Woolf) (4: 195–96). Sometimes such attitudes appear in Woolf's essays and novels, further complicating characterizations of her life and writing. (For further discussion and a range of views on this subject, see, for example, Gerzina; Marcus, "Very Fine"; Whitworth 68–73; Briggs, *Virginia Woolf* 305–10; Seshagiri; Schroder; Lee 308–10; J. Wilson; Cliff.)

THE BLOOMSBURY GROUP

Virginia Woolf's feminist analysis of patriarchy and the bourgeois family and her creation of a new literary prose aesthetic with which she embodied her political insights are perhaps her greatest individual contributions to twentieth-century thought and art. These contributions distinguished her among members of the Bloomsbury Group—a widening circle of visual artists, writers, editors, and cultural critics, who were friends and sometimes collaborators during the first four decades of the twentieth century. In addition to Virginia Woolf, the Group included such figures as the painters Duncan Grant and Vanessa Bell, the economist Maynard Keynes, the writers Lytton Strachey and E. M. Forster, the journalist Desmond MacCarthy, the memoirist Mary MacCarthy, the art critics Roger Fry and Clive Bell, and the political theorist and Labour Party advisor, Leonard Woolf, Virginia Woolf's husband from 1912 until her death in 1941.

In the twenty-first century, Bloomsbury represents a range of contradictory meanings, and its value as a cultural signifier has been thoroughly commodified (Silver, *Virginia Woolf Icon* 149–50, 188). Thus, it is difficult to speak of the Bloomsbury Group as a consistent social entity; its existence as such has even been denied by several of the Group's own members (Hussey, *Virginia Woolf A to Z* 34).

Readers of this book educated within the British system may be familiar with the idea of Bloomsbury as an elitist clique of well-to-do artists and intellectuals who scorned the working classes, the middle classes, politics, and art they had no hand in producing (Nicolson, "Bloomsbury" 8; Swinnerton, *Georgian* 339, 341, 375, 377). This stereotype was most effectively promulgated by the Cambridge lecturer F. R. (Frank Raymond) Leavis and the literary critic and reviewer Queenie Leavis from the post-World War I period through the 1960s (Annan 28–33). Readers educated in the United States may be more likely to associate Bloomsbury with sexual libertinism, especially bisexuality and polyamory, and artistic bohemianism (Silver, *Virginia Woolf Icon* 9, 150, 188–89). Each of these visions oversimplifies a complex set of people whose intersecting lives stimulated boldness and creativity in the arts, social thought, and family arrangements.

In his 1960 memoir, Leonard Woolf describes the shared feeling among a handful of young men who were Cambridge undergraduates at the turn of the century. Their bond was the germ for what would eventually develop into the Bloomsbury Group:

> When in the grim, grey, rainy January days of 1901 Queen Victoria lay dying, we already felt that we were living in an era of incipient revolt and that we ourselves were mortally involved in this revolt against a social system and code of conduct and morality which, for convenience' [sic] sake, may be referred to as bourgeois Victorianism. [. . .] [W]e were struggling against a religious and moral code of cant and hypocrisy which produced and condoned such social crimes and judicial murders as the condemnation of [Alfred] Dreyfus. (*Sowing* 166)

Leonard Woolf, in 1901 a young left-leaning middle-class man who was part of the intellectual elite, expresses his recollection of the turn-of-the-century Zeitgeist in tones that reverberate with Virginia Woolf's critique of the Victorian family. In citing the Dreyfus Affair, Leonard Woolf refers to the 1894 to 1906 episode in European history in which the French army captain Alfred Dreyfus, who was Jewish, was wrongfully sentenced to life imprisonment for treason. The Affair was motivated by anti-Semitism, and in 1898 the French writer Émile Zola intervened on Dreyfus's behalf by publishing "J'accuse . . . !," a public letter of protest to the French president, Felix Faure, for which the state found Zola guilty of libel. Leonard

Woolf's pointed allusion to the Dreyfus Affair in explaining the Cambridge origins of Bloomsbury is rhetorically significant. Zola's letter served as the catalyst for Dreyfus's eventual freedom and the state's recognition of his innocence in 1906 (Working Group; "J'accuse . . . !"). The case illustrates, then, that the novelist's pen has the power to reverse a gross miscarriage of justice and change the course of history. Leonard Woolf's highlighting this historical incident appears intended to provide a weight of political seriousness and concern for social justice that counterbalances caricatures of Bloomsbury as apolitical and self-serving.

Distinct habits of mind more than any unified mindset distinguished this group of friends and fostered among them the desire to come together to discuss ideas and read literature aloud, first at Cambridge University, in the friends' Midnight Society and in the secret debating society the Apostles, and later at the Stephen siblings' new home at 46 Gordon Square in the Bloomsbury district of London (Grant 68; C. Bell 135; L. Woolf, *Sowing* 161–62; *Beginning Again* 23–26). It was 1904. Their father had just died. They were in their early twenties. Woolf's sister, Vanessa Bell, describes the abrupt change of moving from the "gloom and depression" of their father's house to the "exhilarating" atmosphere of "one's own rooms, be[ing] master of one's own time, hav[ing] all the things in fact which come as a matter of course to many of the young today but so seldom then to young women at least" ("Notes on Bloomsbury" 76, 77).

The Stephen sisters' response to this newfound freedom of association meant they had more opportunities to flex their considerable mental and creative powers by widening their intellectual environment. They expanded into previously forbidden territories. Virginia Woolf recalled in her memoir of Bloomsbury the moment when the territory of sexuality was first broached:

He [Lytton Strachey] pointed his finger at a stain on Vanessa's dress.

"Semen?" he said.

Can one really say it? I thought & we burst out laughing. With that one word all barriers of reticence and reserve went down. A flood of the sacred fluid seemed to overwhelm us. Sex permeated our conversation. The word bugger was never far from our lips. We discussed copulation with the same excitement and openness that we had discussed the nature of good. (Qtd. in Q. Bell, *Virginia Woolf* 1: 124)

Bloomsbury gatherings, during which people discussed the abstract and the mundane (V. Bell, "Notes on Bloomsbury" 79), continued on and off at various locales and under different names—Thursday Evenings, the Friday Club, the Memoir Club—from the year 1904 through the 1930s (Leonard Woolf marks the end date for these gatherings as 1956) (L. Woolf, *Downhill* 115; Hussey, *Virginia Woolf A to Z* 34–36; Markert xiv).

"Bloomsberries," as Mary MacCarthy dubbed her friends within this close-knit group, read avidly, making it problematic to reduce the Group's ethos to one or two primary intellectual influences. Nonetheless, George (G. E.) Moore's rigorous intellectual pursuit of the truth and his 1903 philosophical treatise *Principia Ethica*, which the Bloomsbury men had imbibed via the Apostles at Cambridge, was foundational, particularly the last chapter on "The Ideal" (see Hurka; for an opposing view of Moore's influence, see Banfield, *Phantom* 40–41): "By far the most valuable things, which we know or can imagine, are certain states of consciousness, which may be roughly described as the pleasures of human intercourse and the enjoyment of beautiful objects" (G. E. Moore 188). Moore's ethics and, much more generally, Sigmund Freud's discoveries about the unconscious mind contributed to Bloomsbury's interest in exploring the nature of aesthetic value, the internal landscapes of the mind, the limits of friendship, and the frontiers of forthright argument on a panoply of subjects (Rosenbaum, Introduction 1; L. Woolf, *Sowing* 161–64; Holroyd 45–46). Bertrand Russell, who, "[a]long with G. E. Moore, is generally recognized as one of the founders of analytic philosophy" (Irvine), influenced Bloomsbury's philosophizing, particularly as it manifested itself in Woolf's fiction, to a greater degree than even Moore did (Banfield, *Phantom Table* 42, 46). According to Ann Banfield, it was Russell's philosophy, with its emphasis on "perceptions" as the basis of all "empirical evidence" (B. Russell, *Analysis of Matter* 6), "that Woolf . . . came to know as philosophy" (Banfield, *Phantom* 6). Russell's epistemology "addressed the seeming incommensurability of two versions of knowledge of the external world, one direct apprehension of it through the senses and the other scientific knowledge, chiefly modern physics. . . . All we ever know immediately is not matter, but our own sensations" (Banfield,

Phantom 6). As we will see in chapter 3, Russell's ideas take root in Woolf's fiction. Staging a struggle between sense perceptions and scientific truths, *To the Lighthouse* questions the possibility of ascertaining reality beyond human perceptions, which are shown to be constantly in flux.

Following Russell, who wondered in a letter to his lover Lady Ottoline Morrell, "Can human beings *know* anything, and if so what and how?" (*Selected Letters* 404), this community of friends cultivated a fecund intellectual environment based on the agreement that one must "question the truth of everything and the authority of everyone, to regard nothing as sacred" (L. Woolf, *Sowing* 167) and "one need no longer be afraid of saying what one thought" (V. Bell, "Notes on Bloomsbury" 80). Besides freely conversing about sexuality in mix-gendered company and challenging the boundaries of respectability in their sexual relationships, Bloomsbury members innovated, individually and collaboratively, in creating and disseminating art and even in shaping international relations (Markert x–xv). Roger Fry, assisted first by Desmond MacCarthy and later by Leonard Woolf, brought the paintings of Édouard Manet, Vincent van Gogh, Paul Cézanne, Pablo Picasso, Henri Matisse, Paul Gaugin, and other continental European painters to a stunned and confounded English public in his First and Second Post-Impressionist Exhibitions in London in 1910 and 1912, thereby coining a new art movement in England—Post-Impressionism—in the process; in 1913 as part of this movement, Fry established, with Vanessa Bell and Duncan Grant, the Omega Workshops, a decorative arts venture aimed to nurture and financially support English artists interested in Post-Impressionism's emphasis on form and new uses of color (Anscombe 9, 12); Leonard and Virginia Woolf started their own publishing enterprise in 1917, the Hogarth Press, teaching themselves to print on a kitchen tabletop hand-press so as to be able to distribute literature that established publishing houses would not touch, such as Katherine Mansfield's *Prelude* (1918) and T. S. Eliot's *The Waste Land* (1922), and eventually publishing provocative political pamphlets and Freud's complete translated works (L. Woolf, *Beginning* 231–47, 253–55; *Downhill* 161); following Leonard Woolf's involvement in the Fabian Society of socialists in 1913 and the outbreak of World War I in 1914 (and with it, the conscientious objection to conscription of Lytton Strachey, Duncan Grant, E. M. Forster, and Maynard Keynes) (Atkin 23–28, 34–35), Leonard Woolf wrote *International Government* (1916), significant parts of which formed the basis for the International League of Nations and the United Nations (Manson 1–4, 7–9).

VANESSA BELL

Vanessa Stephen Bell, Virginia Woolf's older sister, was a central member of the Bloomsbury circle. From an early age the Stephen sisters dedicated themselves to what would become their life's work: developing their artistic knowledge and craft. For Virginia it was literature; for Vanessa, visual arts. As Woolf's intimate lifelong confidante on par with husband Leonard Woolf, Bell played a significant role in Woolf's life. She also bears a special relationship to Woolf's novel *To the Lighthouse* in that one of the central characters in the novel is a female painter, Lily Briscoe.

Similar to his encouragement of Virginia's interest in reading, Leslie Stephen had supported Vanessa Stephen's artistic inclinations by hiring a drawing teacher for her and later sending her to art school (Spalding 17–19). Between 1896 and 1904, Vanessa received formal training in painting from several schools, including the Royal Academy Schools in London where she studied with John Singer Sargent (Spalding 33–37; Shone 21–28), remembered today for such treasures as *Carnation, Lily, Lily, Rose* (1885–86) at the Tate Museum and *Breakfast in the Loggia* (1910) in the Freer Gallery of Art at the Smithsonian Institution. Another Academy teacher was her cousin Val Prinsep, famous for his commissioned painting of the 1877 Delhi Durbar to proclaim Queen Victoria Empress of India.

Vanessa eventually turned away from formal instruction and the Academy's emphasis on representational (lifelike) art to take charge of her artistic development and individual aesthetic. In 1905 from her home in Bloomsbury, at that time shared with sister Virginia and brothers Thoby and Adrian Stephen, Vanessa began to hold "Friday Club" gatherings to discuss contemporary art with like-minded painters, listen to lectures, and organize occasional exhibitions (Spalding 55–56). She drew inspiration for the bold innovation she would eventually bring to her artwork from a range of influences, including the anti-establishment New English Art Club, trips to Paris, Venice, and Florence, French Impressionism, in particular Henri Matisse's paintings, and Post-Impressionism and the art criticism of Roger Fry (Spalding 40–42, 113, 126–27; Shone 19–29, 36).

"Art," wrote Roger Fry in his *Essay in Aesthetics*, "appreciates emotion in and for itself," and by describing emotion as an "end in itself" Fry was acknowledging the theories of G. E. Moore. . . . In his introduction to the Second Post-Impressionist Exhibition, Fry spelled out the implications of this emphasis on form. "The logical extreme of such a method," he wrote, "would undoubtedly be the attempt to give up all resemblance to natural form, and to create a purely abstract language of form—a visual magic." (Naylor 14, 15)

In addition to co-directing Fry's Omega Workshops, Vanessa Bell, now married to painter and art critic Clive Bell, exhibited her paintings at his Second Post-Impressionist Exhibition in London as well as many other venues. Under the influence of the Omega Workshops, she ventured into the decorative arts, painting furniture, pottery, china, and murals and creating designs for various textiles. To understand the vibrancy and audacity of the Omega aesthetic, as her son Quentin Bell describes, imagine "a stark rectangular vermillion Omega chair, or a flaming yellow ochre and cadmium orange Omega cushion [put beside Edwardian and early Georgian interiors] [and you] would have had the effect of an exploding bomb, a bomb bursting, as it were, with *joie de vivre*" (Q. Bell, "Vanessa Bell" 27).

Virginia Woolf and Vanessa Bell not only appreciated each other's creations, they also seriously scrutinized them and had a hand in their public presentation. For example, Bell designed dust jackets and covers for Woolf's literary works, even illustrating with woodcuts and decorating the pages of some; Woolf in turn composed the foreword to two of Bell's exhibition catalogues (The London Artists' Association, February 1930; LeFevre Galleries, London, March 1934). Critics have documented subtler influences. Woolf's transmutation of childhood memories of their mother into lyrical prose in *To the Lighthouse* may have inspired Bell to paint *The Nursery* (1930–32), "a nostalgic evocation of motherhood" (Spalding 251), and the fireplace tiles depicting a boat sailing to a lighthouse in Woolf's bedroom in Monks House in Rodmell, Sussex (Gillespie, *Sisters'* 157–59). Likewise, Woolf used what she understood of her sister's creative process and finished paintings, including Bell's "obsession with form and colour" and her use of verticals (Morphet 7, 8), as well as her struggles as a female artist to flesh out her painter-character,

Lily, in *To the Lighthouse* (Gillespie, *Sisters'* 107, 195–96, 198–201, 221; Morphet 7, 8, 10–11). Furthermore, both writer and painter grappled with "new problems of structure" (V. Woolf, *Letters* 3: 341 qtd. in Gillespie, *Sisters'* 107) in their art and innovated by rendering individual perceptions and characters abstractly (Gillespie, *Sisters'* 79, 175).

POLITICS

During the period in which Vanessa Bell painted and Virginia Woolf wrote, known as modernism, roughly 1901 to 1945, the political landscape of Britain was changing. The "scramble for Africa" that had occurred in the 1880s had marked an aggressive "New Imperialism" in Britain, which had been reflected ideologically in Queen Victoria's Golden and Diamond Jubilees and the propaganda accompanying the second South African War at the turn of the century (Anglo-Boer War, 1899–1902). By 1900, the British Empire controlled approximately 20 percent of the world's land and people, 50 percent of all war ships, and 40 percent of the world's trade (Ramsden 321–22; Black and MacRaid 236–39; Reynolds 23). Britain's surprisingly drawn-out battle against the Boers in southern Africa, however, had shaken people's confidence in Britain's imperial supremacy.

During the first four decades of the twentieth century, although Britain would reach its strength territorially, it would lose some of its strategic political and economic power to other European nations. Further unsettling British confidence in the new century, World War I (1914–18) was unprecedented in the nature and scope of English casualties. In 1939, with Nazi Germany's invasion of Poland, England entered World War II. And by 1940, after German forces had advanced across much of Europe, they took to the skies above southeast England in a strategic bombing campaign ("The Battle of Britain"), thus bringing the violence to English soil. Woolf experienced these attacks firsthand as her diaries and letters attest: "We have the drone of [German] raiders every night, and the village [of Rodmell] is now fire spotting—"; "We are being a good deal bombed at the moment" (*Letters* 6: 478, 479). The first half of the twentieth century also witnessed the advancement of liberation movements around the world—Pan-Africanism, the Russian Revolution, Englishwomen's suffrage, and India's home rule, to name just a few.

Against the backdrop of these movements, Virginia Woolf's politics have been the subject of fierce debates within Woolf studies for decades. In response to Leonard Woolf's assertion that his wife "was the least political animal that has lived since Aristotle invented the definition" (*Downhill* 27), Nigel Nicolson's claim that "Virginia Woolf held strong political views, but did not possess a political mind" ("Bloomsbury" 20–21), and Quentin Bell's characterization of his aunt as a woman "belong[ing], inescapably, to the Victorian world of Empire, Class and Privilege," for whom "the machinery of politics exasperated and bewildered" (*Virginia Woolf* 2: 186, 188), new generations of feminist scholars, led by Jane Marcus, have extensively documented and analyzed both Woolf's political writings and her practical engagement in politics (see Marcus, "No More Horses"; Black; Lee 667–86). Because the very notion of politics has traditionally been restricted to involvement in government, for centuries the sole purview of men, women's activities of a political nature have often been overlooked in history until the advent of feminist scholarship.

In Woolf's case, her own statements about politics in her published letters may have contributed to her being characterized subsequently as apolitical. For instance, in a 1931 letter to Margaret Llewelyn Davies, General Secretary of the Women's Co-operative Guild, a national organization aimed to improve working-class women's lives, Woolf writes: "I cant [sic] conceive how you politicians can go on being political. All the summer we had nothing but political arguments with Maynard [Keynes] and others; and I finally felt it so completely silly, futile, petty, personal and unreal [. . .] that I retired to my room and read poetry in a rage. [. . .] [I]f everyone read poetry then there'd be no politics; no crisis [. . .] (4: 392). Comments like this one exist side by side others that reflect Woolf's growing feminist consciousness: "I become steadily more feminist [. . .]" (*Letters* 2: 76); "Woman haters depress me [. . .]" (*Diary* 3: 140); "[T]he egotism of men surprises & shocks me even now" (*Diary* 3: 204).

Woolf's political engagements went well beyond thoughts jotted down in her diary and letters, and heated political debates with friends, however. Over the course of her life, she participated in a range of activities—from keeping politically informed through newspapers, radio, and lectures to participating in grass roots work; from joining reform and advocacy groups to signing petitions and volunteering as a lecturer. For example, Woolf had ties to several feminist organizations, the People's Suffrage Federation, the

Women's Co-operative Guild (part of the larger Co-operative movement), and the London and National Society for Women's Service,
as well as with the British Labour Party (Black 184). As for grass
roots actions, in her early twenties Woolf volunteered at a night
school, Morley College, for working-class women and men, where
she taught English history, literature, and composition for nearly two
years; a few years later she was "working for the vote" for women by
addressing envelopes for the People's Suffrage Federation (V. Woolf,
Letters 6: 419; *Passionate* 217, 218, 222, 223; Lee 418–20). In her thir-
ties, she regularly attended conferences and hosted meetings of the
Women's Co-operative Guild; in her fifties, she became treasurer of
the Rodmell Women's Institute, a local branch of the larger non-
partisan Women's Institutes movement (V. Woolf, *Letters* 6: 448).
Throughout her life, although it was work she did not particularly
enjoy, she lectured to various groups and arranged for her friends to
share specialized knowledge with the public as well. Once she was
well known, she lent her name to numerous political causes, including demanding that the British government free an Austrian Jewish
lawyer from England's internment camps as well as end its relations
with Mussolini and support the Spanish Republican government in
its civil war against Francisco Franco (Lee 675–76).

The majority of her energies, however, went toward her writing,
some of which is overtly political. In addition to *A Room of One's
Own*, she published several shorter essays of a political nature
in such periodicals as *The Daily Worker*, *The New Republic*, and
The Atlantic Monthly. And in 1938 she published her feminist pacifist treatise, *Three Guineas*, after being "plagued by the sudden wish
to write an Anti fascist Pamphlet" (V. Woolf, *Diary* 4: 282). Boldly
comparing English patriarchy at home to European fascism abroad,
Woolf argues in *Three Guineas* that sex chauvinism in all of its elaborate manifestations engenders national chauvinism, which precip-
itates empire building and war. If women want to "preserve peace,"
instead of signing petitions, joining organizations, and donating
money, they need to form an "Outsiders' society" whose members
refuse to participate in all patriarchal institutions, including the
church, the university, the military, and the professions (*Three
Guineas* 154, 193).

Woolf believed that persuasive, artful writing on pressing social
issues surpassed government office, street demonstrations, and philanthropy in its potential to improve society; this position does not

make Woolf apolitical nor does it diminish the grass roots work she performed. If we recall the Dreyfus Affair, the writer's willingness to use the pen to engage contemporary social issues can have tremendous political effects. As she explained in her 1940 diary, "Thinking is my fighting" (5: 285).

LOVE AFFAIR WITH VITA SACKVILLE-WEST

If thinking was Virginia Woolf's way of fighting, then writing was Woolf's way of loving (V. Woolf, *Diary* 3: 18). Woolf's novel *Orlando* (1928), written immediately after *To the Lighthouse*, provides a fictionalized account of the English aristocrat Vita Sackville-West, a popular poet, travel writer, and novelist of the 1920s and '30s. Sackville-West's son Nigel Nicolson dubbed *Orlando* "the longest and most charming love letter in literature," recognizing that this literary tribute to his mother sprang from not only Woolf's creative powers but also her ardent romantic love for Sackville-West (*Portrait* 202). Typically unacknowledged in the popular media (though accepted as commonplace by Woolf scholars since the pioneering work of Jane Lilienfeld and Louise DeSalvo) has been the influence of that love on *To the Lighthouse*, written during the affair's most passionate physical phase begun in December 1925. Though not as obviously connected to the novel's characters, setting, and plot as are details about Woolf's parents, her painter-sister, and the family's seaside summers in St. Ives, Woolf's relationship with Sackville-West remains an important biographical context for the novel (Briggs, *Virginia Woolf* 166–70; see, also, Stalla 27, 29, 31).

In Chapter 4, I will discuss specific "lesbian readings" of the novel. Here, I wish to point out some parallels between Woolf's love affair with Sackville-West and her work on *To the Lighthouse*. She wrote *To the Lighthouse* during a period of intense excitement. Woolf found in Sackville-West feminine beauty she felt she herself lacked; bold physicality, as in how Sackville-West strode through life undaunted and surrounded herself with sumptuousness; female companionship and conversation about the craft of writing; exuberant desire and serenity (V. Woolf, *Letters* 3: 266, 306–7; 5: 148; *Diary* 3: 52; see, also, Raitt, *Vita* 149, 158–61). In two letters from 1930 to her friend the composer Ethel Smyth, the first one on the subject of "Perversion" (4: 200) and Woolf's limited sexual attraction to men, Woolf explains what her love for women satisfied in her: "I cannot get my sense of unity and coherency and all that makes me wish to write the Lighthouse etc. unless I am perpetually stimulated. [. . .] [O]f course I get it tremendously from Leonard—but differently—Lord Lord how many things I want—how many different flowers I visit—[. . .]" (4: 200); "It is true that I only want to show off to women. Women alone stir my imagination—[. . .]" (4: 203; see, also, Cook 726–29; DeSalvo, "Lighting" 204).

In Sackville-West, Woolf found the stimulation she needed to complete *To the Lighthouse*, her most ambitious literary project up to that time. She wrote the novel faster, more freely and easily, and with greater absorption than anything else she would write of comparable magnitude (V. Woolf, *Diary* 3: 39, 58–59, 88, 203, 264; *Letters* 3: 232, 241). Sackville-West's allure for Woolf is perhaps best illustrated by the fact that, although Woolf desired more than anything else to be composing *To the Lighthouse*, she could not stop thinking about Sackville-West even during her precious writing hours (*Letters* 3: 254). The love affair-in-progress stimulated the novel and vice versa. Woolf invented pet names for Sackville-West such as "dolphin" and "porpoise" (*Letters* 3: 395, 398, 468), and both women described their mutual ardor using oceanic metaphors in keeping with the coastal setting of *To the Lighthouse* (Briggs, *Virginia Woolf* 167). If Woolf was Sackville-West's "anchor entangled in gold nuggets at the bottom of the sea" (Sackville-West 297), then Sackville-West was Woolf's "lighthouse in clean waters" (*Letters* 3: 319). In *To the Lighthouse* Woolf would explore, among other things, relationships between women, which she had noted in her diary were "so secret & private compared with relations with men. Why not write about it? truthfully?" (2: 320).

CHAPTER 2

LANGUAGE, STYLE AND FORM

I don't believe you can possibly separate expression from thought in an imaginative work.

—*Virginia Woolf, 1925,* Letters *3*

The association between Virginia Woolf and fear is fairly typical and not solely an outgrowth of Edward Albee's 1962 play about family dysfunction, *Who's Afraid of Virginia Woolf?* According to an alumnus of Williams College in Massachusetts, decades before Albee wrote his play Professor John Hawley Roberts, an English professor and novelist who was Woolf's contemporary, held a public lecture at Williams "to introduce the amateur reader" to Woolf's writing (Funke X1). He entitled the lecture "Who's Afraid of Virginia Woolf?"—a nod toward "Who's Afraid of the Big Bad Wolf?"—the song from Disney's 1933 animated short film *The Three Little Pigs* (Funke X1). Woolf scholar Brenda Silver, in her book *Virginia Woolf Icon* (1999), discusses at length a host of fears associated with Woolf's name (102–16). In this chapter, I address the apprehension Professor Roberts presumably references in his lecture's title: the reader's fear of not being able to comprehend Woolf's writing because of the author's unconventional use of language. By reading this guide in tandem with the novel, readers will no longer be intimidated by Woolf's writing, what literary critics have termed the modernist style.

MODERNISM AND STREAM-OF-CONSCIOUSNESS WRITING

Woolf's writing method, in which she focuses on characters' interior thoughts and feelings as they change from moment to moment and with multiple points of view, has led to her being categorized, to her dismay, with such writers as James Joyce and D. H. Lawrence (V. Woolf, *Letters* 4: 402 n1). Literary critics since the early twentieth century have referred to these writers as "modernist" and to their writing style as "stream of consciousness." May Sinclair first used the term "stream of consciousness" in a literary sense in 1918 when she reviewed Dorothy Richardson's initial three installments of her thirteen-volume novel *Pilgrimage* about a young female protagonist, Miriam Henderson: "In this series there is no drama, no situation, no set scene. Nothing happens. It is just life going on and on. It is Miriam Henderson's stream of consciousness going on and on" (Sinclair 58).

The term "stream of consciousness" had been used previously in non-literary contexts as early as the nineteenth century. For example, according to Suzanne Raitt, the biologist William "McDougall imagines [human] consciousness as a kind of perpetual flowing together of minds, a network of streams constantly joining and separating from one another" (*May Sinclair* 220). Later in the century, psychologist William James took up the term to designate the unity and continuity of individual consciousness (Raitt, *May Sinclair* 218). In the present era, we refer to literature as stream of consciousness if its prose idiom attempts to represent the human mind's free flow of thoughts, characteristically in a nonlinear fashion. It is important not to confuse stream of consciousness with another literary technique, popularized in the 1920s by the Surrealists, "automatic writing." With automatic writing in order to tap into the unconscious, an author writes down the unedited flow of thoughts immediately as they form in the mind when in a state of semi-consciousness, such as upon first waking. Although the former term designates a representation of mental flow and the latter actually records such flow, both terms reflect the keen interest during the early twentieth century in investigating people's interior lives and their multiple states of consciousness, an outgrowth of the relatively new discipline of psychology. Despite how quickly Woolf wrote *To the Lighthouse*, her approach to composing the novel was not an exercise in automatic writing. She based the novel on a preconceived plan, composed it in a conscious state, and painstakingly drafted and revised her manuscript in an attempt to make her prose match her aesthetic vision (Dick, Introduction. To the Lighthouse: *The Original Holograph Draft* 29).

In addition to exploring a character's interior mind, modernist writers often play with point of view by narrating the same events from multiple characters' perspectives. Two examples of this are William Faulkner's *The Sound and the Fury* (1929) in which each chapter is told from a different character's perspective and James Joyce's *Ulysses* (1922) in which point of view changes frequently between and within chapters, and the language used reflects multiple dialects, which shift dramatically as well.

One reason for Woolf's dismay at being grouped together with her male contemporaries Joyce and Lawrence was that their focus on bodies and sex offended her from an artistic standpoint. As she put it, one "[m]ust get out of the way of thinking that indecency is more real than anything else—a dodge now because of the veil of reticence, but a cheap one" (V. Woolf, "Modern Novels (Joyce)" 644). Joyce's writing bored her (*Letters* 3: 80) though she admired the "occasional beauty of his phrases" and envied the critical esteem in which her contemporaries, such as T. S. Eliot, held him ("Modern Novels (Joyce)" 642; *Diary* 2: 69, 202–3). She thought Joyce's writing inferior to hers and, *Ulysses* in particular, pretentious, repulsive, and too reliant on stunts and shock value ("Modern Novels (Joyce)" 643; *Diary* 2: 199–200). She respected Lawrence's literary honesty yet found his "brood[ing] over sex" tiresome (*Letters* 2: 476). More importantly, she believed she was accomplishing something quite original and distinct from the work of these male contemporaries.

For Woolf the issue of gendered writing is complex and fraught. In "Romance and the Heart," a 1923 book review of Dorothy Richardson's novel *Revolving Lights*, the seventh volume of *Pilgrimage*, Woolf praises Richardson for having "developed [. . .] a sentence which we might call the psychological sentence of the feminine gender. [. . .] It is a woman's sentence, but only in the sense that it is used to describe a woman's mind by a writer who is neither proud nor afraid of anything that she may discover in the psychology of her sex" (367). In *A Room of One's Own* (1929), Woolf calls on women to develop a sentence of their own because imitating styles established by great male writers suited neither women's lived experiences nor the living conditions under which they wrote. Woolf's idea of a woman's sentence was meant to function in *A Room of One's Own* as a metaphor to help expose the drastically unequal social conditions under which women and men lived and created art. Woolf was keenly aware of the barrier women writers faced in being taken seriously by the male-dominated literary establishment; therefore, her emphasizing the feminineness of women's writing was inherently risky.

As a case in point, although avant-gardist Wyndham Lewis also thought stream of consciousness "a feminine phenomenon" (138), rather than celebrate it as a sign of contemporary art's vigor, he associated it—via emasculation, homosexuality, and decadence—with aesthetic decay (104, 139, 140).

THE NOVEL'S STRUCTURE

Knowing what Woolf planned for the structure of *To the Lighthouse* and what she aimed to achieve with her writing methods will help the reader navigate the novel's formal and syntactic vortices. In an early draft of "How Should One Read A Book?," Woolf's lecture to girls at the Hayes Court Common school in Kent on 30 January 1926 and composed while writing *To the Lighthouse*, she instructs the reader "to teach oneself how to read" books by "taking the writer's sentences, one after another, & building them up in the shape he intended" ("How" [Sept. 1925] 55, 56 [MS 1.87, 1.89]). Her emphasis on a book's shape is significant. Woolf sought to write literature that not so much told a story, that is, emphasized plot and dramatic action, but rather created impressions with language that would elicit intense sensations in the reader. Those impressions, piled one on top of the other, would, Woolf believed, form a shape in the mind's eye. In some ways this goal paralleled what the Post-Impressionist visual artists like Vanessa Bell were attempting to achieve in their paintings where form and color, even paint application methods, trumped realistic renderings of subject matter.

To the Lighthouse is divided into three distinct sections of varying lengths: "The Window" (roughly 125 pages), "Time Passes" (roughly 20 pages), and "The Lighthouse" (roughly 60 pages). From beginning to end, the events of the novel occur over a period of ten years; however, the first and third sections each take place during the span of only one day. The middle section, "Time Passes," covers a ten-year period that is punctuated by the historical occasion of the Great War (1914–18). Months before Woolf began composing *To the Lighthouse*, she traced a thick, squat "H" shape in her notebook with the caption "Two blocks joined by a corridor" (To the Lighthouse: *Original* 48 [MS 11]). A month before she began writing, she fleshed out in her diary what the shape stood for: "(I conceive the book in 3 parts: 1. at the drawing room window; 2. seven years passed [which she subsequently changed to ten]; 3. the voyage:)" (3: 36).

This shape represents not only the book's organization, that is, that it will have three sections, but also more importantly Woolf's plan that the middle section would be distinct; it stands alone as a long, narrow corridor connecting "The Window" to "The Lighthouse." In concrete terms, this middle section of the book covers the longest stretch of time (ten years), yet the fewest pages are devoted to it (approximately twenty). Conversely, the beginning and end sections, which cover the shortest period of time (one day each), are given the most pages (185 combined). The book's middle corridor, then, condenses time while the other two sections expand it. Woolf structured *To the Lighthouse* this way because she wanted to disturb fixed ideas about the passage of time and experiment with the limits of prose fiction's representational capacities. In the "Passages for Further Study" section below, I will discuss Woolf's time experiment in greater detail as I suggest ways to approach reading "Time Passes."

As she began drafting *To the Lighthouse*, Woolf revised her initial outline, adding more information about the novel's characters. For example, in the following passage about "The Window," Woolf moves from delineating structure to discussing larger stylistic concerns as well as plot and thematic details:

> The plan of this book is roughly that it shall consist of three parts: one, Mrs. Ramsay (?) sitting at the window: while Mr. R. walks up & down in the dusk: [. . .] there shall be curves of conversation or reflection or description [. . .] modulated by his appearance & disappearance at the window: gradually it shall grow later; the child shall go to bed; the engaged couple shall appear: [. . .] My aim being to find a unit [. . .] for the sentence which shall be less emphatic & intense than that in Mrs. D: [*Mrs. Dalloway*] [. . .] To precipitate feeling, there should be a sense of waiting, of expectation. [. . .] (To the Lighthouse: *Original* TTL/Page 2 [MS 1.5])

Here Woolf illustrates her primary writing concerns in composing *To the Lighthouse*: to create a new kind of sentence to convey obliquely the multiple effects one character has on another and, at the same time, to transmit shifts in feeling in the characters and also elicit them in the reader.

GENRE AND STYLE

Because for Woolf "a novel is an impression not an argument" (*Letters* 5: 91), her objectives have little to do with conveying a message or telling a good story. Nor was she content to use existing writing styles to achieve her aims. Even the genre of the novel seemed ill-fitted to her experiments in prose fiction writing: "([. . .] I have an idea that I will invent a new name for my books to supplant 'novel.' A new—by Virginia Woolf. But what? Elegy?)" (*Diary* 3: 34). An elegy is a mournful song to lament the dead, in this case, Woolf's parents, Leslie and Julia Stephen. The elegy is also a poetic form. Compare elegy to eulogy, a speech of praise about the dead, and one will see that elegy was an apt term to describe the form of *To the Lighthouse*, what Woolf later referred to as one of her "serious poetic experimental books" (*Diary* 3: 131). Her use of the term "elegy" matches not merely the subject matter of the book—her deceased parents—but also even more importantly Woolf's struggle "to find a unit [. . .] for the sentence" that was closer to poetry than to prose.

Two analogies for this new type of sentence reappear in letters and diary entries written throughout her life: music and water. "I always think of my books as music before I write them" (*Letters* 6: 426), Woolf explains to poet Stephen Spender in 1940, and she repeatedly describes literary style as "all rhythm" (*Letters* 3: 247). Woolf rejected the Edwardian writers' "formal railway line of sentence" that moves steadily along its track from point a. to b. because "people don't and never did feel or think or dream for a second in that way [. . .]" (*Letters* 3: 135, 136). She preferred a sentence that moved rhythmically as water does, flowing and eddying in a stream or rising and crashing in waves; she understood its greater potential to represent human perception (*Letters* 1: 247, 383). In keeping with her idea that novel writing was closest to composing music, Woolf arranged in "making up 'To the Lighthouse'—[for] the sea [. . .] to be heard all through it" (*Diary* 3: 34).

The musical composition analogy made sense to Woolf because she wanted to compose literature in such a way as to give voice to multiple lines of thought and feeling simultaneously. Like the complex textures of a line of polyphonic music, prose that is liberated from the restraint of conventional syntax might evoke the multiple perceptions and points of view that exist not only from multiple characters' perspectives but also within a single character, whose sensations alter in response to every passing stimulus. Thus, it follows that Woolf "should like to write four lines at a time, describing the same feeling, as a musician does; because it always seems to me that things are going on at so many different levels simultaneously" (*Letters* 5: 315). Only by creating a prose style that allowed such freedom could she then explore the depths of human consciousness—rather than describe the surface realities, as, Woolf lamented, the previous generation of writers had done.

To develop such a prose style, she experimented with a range of linguistic and literary elements, including punctuation, syntax, and point of view. She wondered, for instance, if parentheses could be used to convey "the sense of reading the two things at the same time?" and therefore not "lose the intensity of the moment" (*Diary* 3: 106). Woolf's use of the punctuation marks of parentheses, as well as brackets and parenthetical, that is, qualifying, phrases more generally, is pervasive throughout *To the Lighthouse*. These long and frequent parenthetical phrases may be difficult for a first-time reader of Woolf. Her desire to convey the "intensity of the moment"—what she calls elsewhere "moments of being" after Thomas Hardy's "moments of vision" (*Diary* 3: 105, 106)—distinguishes her writing from the Edwardian novelists Arnold Bennett, John Galsworthy, and Aldous Huxley. "Moments of being" for Woolf include brief bursts of feeling, sensation, or understanding in the interior lives of her characters. From the perspectives of those outside the character experiencing these sensations, such moments appear insignificant, even nonexistent. In describing these moments to herself in her diary, she contrasts them with "the automatic customary unconscious" ways of being in the world, laden as human society is with convention and routine (3: 105). In her essays "Mr. Bennett and Mrs. Brown" (1923) and "Modern Fiction" (1925), Woolf proposes that modern writers are attempting to translate into fiction these moments of heightened consciousness.

Woolf's focus on heightened states of consciousness as well as the distinction she makes between them and "the automatic customary unconscious" mind suggests French philosopher Henri Bergson's concept of "duration" ("*la durée*"), a favorite critical focus for modernist scholars of the 1950s and '60s (Goldman, "Modernist" 45–46; see, for example, Kumar; Hafley). According to Bergson, human consciousness is not unified and spatial but instead comprised of multiple "interpenetrat[ing]" perceptions and memories experienced temporally as a "continuous," "indivisible" flow (Lawlor and Moulard).

He contrasts this concept of "duration" with "extensity"—that is, "physical phenomena," which we perceive in the external world (Bergson 224, 228). According to Bergson,

> there are finally two different selves, one of which is . . . the external projection of the other, its . . . social representation. We reach the former by deep introspection, which leads us to grasp our inner states as living things, constantly *becoming*. . . . The greater part of the time we live outside ourselves, hardly perceiving anything of ourselves but our own ghost. . . . Hence . . . we live for the external world rather than for ourselves. . . . (231)

The first four paragraphs of *To the Lighthouse* illustrate Woolf's attempt to represent in writing such "inner states," those "moments of intensity," and her use of parentheses to convey the simultaneity of events. The opening scene depicts the musings of a young boy, James Ramsay, who is cutting out pictures from a store catalogue while his mother looks on. The novel begins *in medias res* with Mrs. Ramsay responding to James's question about whether he will be taken for a sail to the lighthouse the next day. His mother suggests the affirmative; his father dissents. James's emotions quickly shift from profound joy to intense hatred.

The second sentence of the novel's second paragraph offers an oblique explanation of Woolf's concept of "moments of being": "any turn in the wheel of sensation has the power to crystallize and transfix the moment upon which its gloom or radiance rests" (3). Six-year-old James Ramsay, Woolf tells us, "belonged [. . .] to that great clan" (3) of people who are especially sensitive to subtle mood changes taking place around them and whose volatile emotional states and tremendous imaginative capacities—after all James has the ability to imbue a paper cut-out and an idea of a journey with mythic importance—make the unseen world more real to them than the material or empirical world ruled by dispassionate reason. The visible world is where his father resides. Thus Mr. Ramsay, deaf to his son's need to be let down tenderly, pragmatically declares that the weather will not permit the longed for journey.

Woolf seems to suggest in the novel's opening passages that for a character to experience the intensity of "the moment" "transfix[ed]" he or she must, like James Ramsay, be particularly sensitive and reflective. Although this may hold true generally in Woolf's writing, other modernist writers devised their own versions of "moments of being" and granted them to characters who, even for a moment, stopped moving through life autonomically to take time to reflect. So, for example, in *Dubliners* (1914), James Joyce frequently depicts brash protagonists being struck at the end of stories with "epiphanies," during which the characters' own arrogance is revealed (as in "Araby" and "The Dead").

In the last sentence of *To the Lighthouse*'s second paragraph, Woolf achieves her objective to use parentheses, that is, intervening nonessential phrases and clauses set off by commas, in order to represent multiple layers of perception in a single sentence:

> The wheelbarrow, the lawnmower, the sound of poplar trees, leaves whitening before rain, rooks cawing, brooms knocking, dresses rustling—*all these were so coloured and distinguished in his mind that he had already his private code*, his secret language, though he appeared the image of stark and uncompromising severity, with his high forehead and his fierce blue eyes, impeccably candid and pure, frowning slightly at the sight of human frailty, so that his mother, watching him guide his scissors neatly round the refrigerator [that he was cutting out from the Army and Navy Stores catalogue], imagined him all red and ermine on the [law] Bench or directing a stern and momentous enterprise in some crisis of public affairs. (3–4; emphasis added)

I have used italics to indicate which part of the sentence above is the independent clause, that is, it contains the essential elements of the sentence: "all these were so coloured and distinguished in his mind that he had already his private code." Everything else is parenthetical, interrupting or preceding the central clause, either to elaborate or offer opposing information on the ideas expressed therein. The clause, although narrated by an omniscient third-person narrator, reflects James's point of view. He thinks about the things in life he treasures, things he associates with his mother: "[t]he wheelbarrow, the lawnmower, the sound of poplar trees, leaves whitening before rain, rooks cawing, brooms knocking, dresses rustling." What follows this clause, however, is told from another perspective. James is inside his own head, using "his private code, his secret language" to communicate with himself. He is not outside his head observing his appearance, that is, "his high forehead and his fierce blue eyes."

An example of free indirect discourse (Childers and Hentzi 118), the third-person narration describing James's attributes blends with what appear to be Mrs. Ramsay's actual thoughts about her son. She sees in her son's face the promise of future professional achievement, either in law or politics. Thus, in a single sentence filled with intricate asides, Woolf gives the reader two distinct characters' points of view seemingly in the same instant.

NARRATION AND POINT OF VIEW

Although a third-person omniscient narrator tells the story moving in and out of multiple characters' minds, as described above, Woolf's handling of point of view is further complicated by the fact that characters' perspectives, especially their views on other characters, change frequently throughout the novel, sometimes within a paragraph or even a single sentence. This approach to narration, which critic Erich Auerbach describes as the "'multipersonal representation of consciousness'" (469–74), is something Woolf strived to achieve because she thought it accurately reflected the multiplicity and unpredictability of human perspectives. As Susan Dick explains after closely studying Woolf's original writing notebooks containing the first draft of *To the Lighthouse* and its subsequent revisions, "[w]hen revising the book, one method she [Woolf] used to make it more dramatic was to refine the point of view in it. . . . The marvelous interplay between characters observed and characters observing, which we enjoy because of the shifting points of view, is often not present in the first draft" (Introduction. To the Lighthouse: *The Original* 22).

Furthermore, a character's thoughts often flow into those of other characters, making it difficult sometimes for the reader to determine where one character's thoughts leave off and another character's begin. The overall effect is not a single stream of consciousness but rather multiple tributaries feeding into a larger mental sea, thus mirroring the theory of consciousness of nineteenth-century biologist William McDougall, discussed above. We see this happening in a later scene from "The Window" in which the Ramsays and their guests, graduate student Charles Tansley and painter Lily Briscoe, engage in conversations at the dinner table over a meal of Bœuf en Daube:

> What damned rot they talk, thought Charles Tansley, laying down his spoon precisely in the middle of his plate, which he had swept clean, as if, Lily thought (he sat opposite to her with his back to

the window precisely in the middle of view), he were determined to make sure of his meals. [. . .]

"Do you write many letters, Mr. Tansley?" asked Mrs. Ramsay, pitying him too, Lily supposed; for that was true of Mrs. Ramsay—she pitied men always as if they lacked something—women never, as if they had something. He wrote to his mother; otherwise he did not suppose he wrote one letter a month, said Mr. Tansley, shortly.

For he was not going to talk the sort of rot these people wanted him to talk. He was not going to be condescended to by these silly women. (85)

The perspective of Charles Tansley, Mr. Ramsay's protégé, begins and ends this passage: what rot these Ramsays and their friends talk, for Tansley is from the lower middle classes and feels he does not fit in here at the Ramsays' dinner table with their genteel manners and superficial conversation. Quickly, however, Tansley's perspective gives way to Lily's perspective on Tansley—at first, he's pedantic and boorish, then, he has such penetrating blue eyes—and thus complicates the reader's view of him. Does Mrs. Ramsay actually pity men and admire women, or does Lily merely read this into Mrs. Ramsay's remark? Perhaps the former, as Tansley also senses something amiss in Mrs. Ramsay's remarks, condescension, and so perfunctorily answers her direct question and then retreats into his private thoughts and the comfort of a chauvinist conviction that "Women made civilisation impossible [. . .]" (85).

INTERTEXTUALITY

Another aspect of the language in *To the Lighthouse* is Woolf's incorporation of weighty-sounding yet seemingly disconnected lyrical phrases sometimes set off in block quotes on the page. Three of the main sources are the poems "The Charge of the Light Brigade" (1854) by Alfred Lord Tennyson, "A Garden Song" ["Luriana, Lurilee"] (1945) by Charles Elton, and "The Castaway" (1803) by William Cowper. As with the sounds of the sea Woolf wanted to be heard in *To the Lighthouse*, spoken lines of poetry and prose from these and other literary sources resound throughout the novel. Parts of William Shakespeare's "Sonnet 98," Percy B. Shelley's "To Jane: The Invitation," and William Browne's "The Sirens' Song" also make an appearance (Hussey, *To the Lighthouse* 223, 229). Most often

Mr. Ramsay, the book's philosopher-father, interjects them into conversations. These poetic fragments appear to echo the soundscape of Virginia Stephen's childhood. For Woolf had planned that at "the centre [of *To the Lighthouse*] is father's character, sitting in a boat, reciting We perished, each alone, while he crushes a dying mackerel—[. . .]" (*Diary* 3: 18–19).

"We perished, each alone" appears in the novel's final section, "The Lighthouse" (165, 169, 191, 207). Mr. Ramsay and his children, Cam and James, finally take their voyage to the lighthouse—accompanied by a fisherman and his son, who cuts a chunk of flesh for bait from a live fish before tossing it back into the sea (180; see D. Wilson; Goldman, *Feminist*). The poetic source is Cowper's "The Castaway," an elegy about a seaman's drowning, based on an event depicted in an eighteenth-century travel narrative, Lord George *Anson's Voyage Round the World* (1748) (Chantler). The poem's speaker uses the occasion of his crewmate's death to strike a tone, in the poem's final stanza, of melancholia over man's aloneness in the face of his mortality. It is an apt line to have the father character utter in *To the Lighthouse*, Woolf's elegy on Leslie and Julia Stephen. Woolf may have put her father's memory to rest upon finishing *To the Lighthouse*, but a year after it was published she could still "hear his voice" (*Diary* 3: 208)—the voice of the "unworldly, very distinguished and lonely" agnostic Leslie Stephen ("Sketch" 158).

As with most things about this novel, however, the autobiographical connection is just the beginning of the meaning of these intertextual passages (see Doyle, "These Emotions" 58–59; "Voyaging" 161–62). "We perished, each alone," first spoken by Mr. Ramsay, recurs later on the lips and in the minds of Cam and James. Together with two other lines repeated in this section, "*But I beneath a rougher sea / Was whelmed in deeper gulfs than he*" (166, 206), the final couplet of Cowper's poem, these poetic fragments form a fugue of sonorous sound that suggests continuity and harmony even as the storyline represents life as chaotic and filled with strife.

The poetic fragments also accent themes present in the storyline. In the most basic sense, both poem and novel recount a historic sea voyage. "The Castaway" recounts a trip around the world that was fraught with disaster and soul searching. Thus, it provides an objective correlative for the seemingly undramatic events that transpire in the boat between Mr. Ramsay and his two youngest children. Literary accounts of epic voyages—both Cowper's and Lord Anson's—elevate by association, and also at the same time gently mock, the mundane concerns of middle-class family life (see S. Friedman). As if to make this point, "The Window" section of *To the Lighthouse* contains a line from another poem, William Browne's "Sirens' Song"—"*Steer, hither steer your winged pines, all beaten Mariners*" (119)—the title of which references an incident in King Odysseus's heroic ten-year voyage home after the Trojan War depicted in Homer's sixth-century Greek epic *The Odyssey*.

In a similar though more focused manner, individual poetic fragments resonate contrapuntally to sound out a character's state of mind. For example, when Mr. Ramsay murmurs, "'But I beneath a rougher sea,'" he is imagining himself living without Mrs. Ramsay, "walking on the terrace, alone" (166):

> Sitting in the boat, he bowed, he crouched himself, acting instantly his part—the part of a desolate man, widowed, bereft; [. . .] [He] staged for himself as he sat in the boat, a little drama; which required of him decrepitude and exhaustion and sorrow [. . .] and then there was given him in abundance women's sympathy, and he imagined how they would soothe him and sympathise with him, and [. . .] he sighed and said gently and mournfully,
> But I beneath a rougher sea
> Was whelmed in deeper gulfs than he. [. . .] (166)

Here Woolf uses fragments of Cowper's poem not only to poke fun at her character Mr. Ramsay but also to show him self-consciously mocking himself for his histrionics. These literary interpolations operate as another kind of parenthesis. They appear to throw a sentence or a scene offtrack; yet, they actually allow Woolf to burrow deeper into her material.

Not all of Woolf's literary sources are especially lofty, however. In fact one of the novel's most fascinating intertextual insertions is from the Grimms' fairytale "The Fisherman and His Wife." In the original story, a fisherman catches an enchanted flounder, which he releases back into the ocean. Upon hearing of this, the man's wife demands that her husband ask the flounder to grant them a series of wishes retroactively in exchange for the flounder's freedom. Each of the wife's wishes—she desires a nicer home and greater social status—is more grandiose than the one before, and the fisherman repeats the following refrain:

Flounder, flounder, in the sea,
Come, I pray thee, here to me;
For my wife, good Ilsabil,
Wills not as I'd have her will. (V. Woolf, *To the Lighthouse* 56)

The wife is never satisfied with what the flounder grants them because she can always imagine something grander. The tale's moral is that wanting that which eludes one in life leads to perpetual dissatisfaction. Interestingly, it is also a cautionary connubial myth about a brow-beaten husband under the thumb of a greedy and selfish woman.

In the first section of *To the Lighthouse*, Mrs. Ramsay reads the fairytale to her son James. In between passages from the Brothers Grimm, Woolf interweaves Mrs. Ramsay's thoughts about her husband's behavior—specifically his constant demand from her for reassurance and emotional sustenance—and what such behavior says about their marriage:

> It was sympathy he wanted, to be assured of his genius, first of all, and then to be taken within the circle of life, warmed and soothed, to have his senses restored to him, his barrenness made fertile, and all the rooms of the house made full of life—. [. . .] [S]he assured him, beyond a shadow of a doubt, by her laugh, her poise, her competence [. . .] that it was real; the house was full; the garden blowing. [. . .] So boasting of her capacity to surround and protect, there was scarcely a shell of herself left for her to know herself by; all was so lavished and spent. [. . .]
>
> Immediately, Mrs. Ramsay seemed to fold herself together, [. . .] and the whole fabric fell in exhaustion upon itself, so that she had only strength enough to move her finger, in exquisite abandonment to exhaustion, across the page of Grimm's fairy story, while there throbbed through her, [. . .] the rapture of successful creation. [. . .] Yet, as the resonance died, and she turned to the Fairy Tale again, Mrs. Ramsay felt not only exhausted in body [. . .] but also there tinged her physical fatigue some faintly disagreeable sensation with another origin. Not that, as she read aloud the story of the Fisherman's Wife, she knew precisely what it came from; nor did she let herself put into words her dissatisfaction when she realised, at the turn of the page when she stopped and heard dully, ominously, a wave fall, how it came from this: she did not like, even for a second, to feel finer than her husband; and

further, could not bear not being entirely sure, when she spoke to him, of the truth of what she said. (37, 38, 39)

This is a long, complicated passage about the bargains Mrs. Ramsay has struck to support her husband and maintain their marriage: the emotional exhaustion, the imbalances of power, the suppressed feelings of disappointment and resentment, and the little lies oft repeated. At the same time, Mrs. Ramsay revels in her creative powers, her ability to transform into grandeur the once brilliant but now more often barren, emotionally stunted man.

The parallels between Mr. and Mrs. Ramsay's story and "The Fisherman and His Wife" are numerous and intriguing. (For a variety of interpretations, see N. Friedman; Pedersen; Blotner; Henke; D. Wilson; Marcus, "Taking"; Goldman, *Feminist*.) Mrs. Ramsay fulfills the role of both the fisherman bullied by his mate and the enchanted flounder who grants the spouse his or her wish and transforms meager households into beautiful palaces in which "all the rooms of the house [were] made full of life" (V. Woolf, *To the Lighthouse* 37). And yet, in both stories something about the situation, it seems to the fisherman and Mrs. Ramsay, does not feel quite right.

Another less obvious parallel exists between the Fisherman's Wife and the young James Ramsay from the beginning of *To the Lighthouse*. The Fisherman's Wife, on whom the enchanted flounder bestows a series of houses and, eventually, monarchical and religious titles, can never enjoy the present moment or even appreciate her newfound riches because she always compares her present situation to potential loftier future ones. Similarly, James Ramsay "cannot keep this feeling separate from that, but must let future prospects, with their joys and sorrows, cloud what is actually at hand" (3). Both characters let what could have been moments of supreme joy evaporate because they cannot live fully in the moment.

PASSAGES FOR FURTHER STUDY

Time Passes

Conceived of as the corridor that joins "The Window" to "The Lighthouse," "Time Passes" is unlike the rest of the novel. It is brief, highly compressed, and, in terms of language, even more experimental than the other two sections. In her diaries and letters, Woolf expresses repeatedly her anxiety and doubts about "Time Passes," "the most difficult abstract piece of writing" (*Diary* 3: 76) she had embarked on in her most experimental novel to date. "Is it nonsense, is it brilliance?," she wondered (*Diary* 3: 76). In chapter 4, I will describe how reviewers have responded to this question as well as what literary critics have interpreted this section of the novel to mean. In chapter 3, I will provide a close analysis of specific portions of "Time Passes." Here, I want to focus on what Woolf intended this section of the novel to accomplish, why she wrote it the way she did, and what strategies readers new to Woolf can employ in order for them to be able to make sense of "Time Passes" for themselves.

If we concur with Woolf's suggestion, quoted in the epigraph to this chapter, that one cannot "possibly separate expression from thought in an imaginative work" (*Letters* 3: 201), then her goal to portray the passage of ten years in twenty pages after devoting 125 pages to a single day would reasonably require a new stylistic approach. Woolf describes this section of the novel as representing "the flight of time," and she conceives of it as "this impersonal thing" (*Diary* 3: 36) almost entirely devoid of dialogue and human interaction: "an empty house, no people's characters, the passage of time, all eyeless & featureless with nothing to cling to" (*Diary* 3: 76).

Woolf had already experimented with stretching out time in *Mrs. Dalloway* (1925), devoting a nearly 300–page novel to one day in the life of her protagonist, Clarissa Dalloway. And she was not the first writer of her era to experiment in this manner. James Joyce, in his landmark novel *Ulysses*, described one day in the life of his anti-hero, Leopold Bloom, in nearly 650 pages. What was the impetus for these modernist experiments with time?

Around the same period that Freud's theories of the unconscious and psychosexual development were revolutionizing popular notions of the self and raising questions about the mind—what are the limits of the knowable? how much control do we have over what we desire?—Albert Einstein's discoveries about the properties of matter, space, and time were shaking up conventional perceptions of how the universe functions. In particular, his 1905 and 1915 Special and General Theories of Relativity toppled the established belief that time moved always at the same speed, that is, that it was constant. In fact, using the mathematical equation $E = mc^2$, Einstein proved that for objects moving at the speed of light (approximately 186,000 miles per second), time stands still; therefore, the velocity with which an object moves changes the properties of time that govern that object.

If something as reliably constant as the passage of time, which orders our daily existence and gives shape and meaning to our lives, is actually variable, then how can we depend on other seeming constants with which we make sense of the world? The doubts that such scientific discoveries produced in people during the early twentieth century helped galvanize many artists to explore new forms and initiate new approaches in art.

Woolf asserts in her diary that her motivation for writing "Time Passes" was that she was "dared to do [it] by my friends" although in a more serious vein she also admits that this section of the novel "interests me very much. A new problem like that breaks fresh ground in ones [sic] mind; prevents the regular ruts" (3: 36). As a reader, one might read "Time Passes" with this same attitude. It provides a "new problem" to the reader accustomed to novels in which characters, propelled by human-like motivations, act in concrete ways within the parameters of space and time already established within the novel.

One possible solution to the problem posed by "Time Passes" is to read it as if it were a prose poem, focusing on the rhythms and repeated sounds of the language, the imagery and metaphors, and the allusions to subjects outside the novel. Woolf in fact considered these pages to be "the lyric portions" of *To the Lighthouse* (*Diary* 3: 106). In a letter to Vita Sackville-West, she wrote, "I was doubtful about Time Passes. It was written in the gloom of the Strike [1926 General Strike in England]: then I re-wrote it: then I thought it impossible as prose—I thought you could have written it as poetry" (3: 374). It was Woolf herself who wrote it as poetry, however. Her original writing notebook contains a loose page of an outline for "Time Passes" that reads like a poem:

> Now the question of the ten years. [. . .]
> The Seasons.
> The Skull
> The gradual dissolution of everything
> This is to be contrasted with the permanence of—what?
> Sun, moon & stars.
> Hopeless gulfs of misery. [. . .]
> The War.
> Change. Oblivion. Human vitality. Old woman
> Cleaning up. [. . .]
> We are handed on by our children ? [. . .]

The devouringness of nature.
But all the time, this passes. [. . .] (To the Lighthouse:
  Original 51 [MS 1.1])

The unifying theme of "Time Passes" is stated in the third and fourth lines: the struggle between "dissolution" and "permanence" in life. In the prose version of "Time Passes," the forces of dissolution are represented by nature's elements—wind, rain, waves—aided by time itself as well as manmade destructive powers—the conflicts and armaments of World War I. Conversely, the forces of permanence are light—"[s]un, moon & stars"—represented by the lighthouse beam— and loveliness—the human need for beauty. Although individuals pass away, and in "Time Passes" there are several deaths recorded as parenthetical asides, the memories of beloved people, albeit fragile, endure. Such memories are "handed on by our children" and others; they represent a permanent record of "[h]uman vitality."

The battle between "dissolution" and "permanence" mentioned in the outline for "Time Passes" is being waged throughout *To the Lighthouse*, especially between "The Window" section and "Time Passes." "The Window" documents one day in the lives of a cluster of people, the Ramsays and some of their friends. Their day is filled with many moments, and, despite their ordinariness, the intensity and significance of these moments are shown, aided by Woolf's parenthetical style and the section's length. Yet, as with most days, such moments end without leaving a permanent record. By contrast, "Time Passes" documents larger forces at work in the world that affect an infinite number of people over an extended period of time: the changing seasons, decay and new growth, floods and winds, loss of memory and death, empire and war, and the search for answers to metaphysical questions—what is truth? beauty? life's meaning?

DISCUSSION QUESTIONS

1. The two other main poetic sources quoted in *To the Lighthouse*, Tennyson's "The Charge of the Light Brigade" and Elton's "A Garden Song" ["Luriana, Lurilee"], also operate on multiple levels to enrich the novel. Using the example above as a model, see if you can determine how poetic fragments from each of these works function in a given scene, either to accent themes or counterpoint a character's state of mind. You can accomplish this best if you begin by reading

the poems in their entirety. Complete texts of Tennyson's, Elton's, and Cowper's poems are available online, and you can even listen to Tennyson's and Cowper's poems read aloud at http://www.archive. org/details/audio_poetry. Tennyson's poem pays tribute to the famous Battle of Balaclava during the Crimean War (1854–55), during which over one hundred British cavalry were killed. The poem by the lesser-known Elton, which was published in 1900 nearly fifty years after Elton's death, describes the garden at Clevedon Court, the Elton family's hereditary estate in Somerset, and, most likely, suggests the poet's love for his cousin Laura Beatrice Elton (Shaw 90–91). Before turning back to Woolf's novel, determine the tone of each poem, highlighting the words each poet uses to create this tone. Consider, too, how the poem's rhythm affects its tone.

Beginning with the Tennyson poem, read chapters 3 through 6 of "The Window" section of *To the Lighthouse.* Tennyson's line *"Stormed at with shot and shell"* appears on page 17, and the line *"Some one had blundered"* recurs on several subsequent pages. Mr. Ramsay is reciting Tennyson in this section, and the poetic fragments and the manner in which he delivers them suggest something about him as a character. What is the mood of each scene? Whose point of view prevails? What do the poetic fragments mean in this new context? What, if anything, has shifted, and why?

Once you have teased out the ways Tennyson's lines reverberate within Woolf's, repeat this exercise with Elton's poem, focusing on the end of chapter 7 through chapter 19 of "The Window" (pages 107 to 124).

2. In "Time Passes" there are two sets of characters depicted, one previously introduced in "The Window," the Ramsay family and their guests, and the other, the charwomen, Mrs. McNab and Mrs. Bast. Discuss Woolf's differing treatment of these sets of characters in "Time Passes" in relation to the other "actors" in this section, that is, the airs, the lighthouse beam, the rain, and so on. What effect do the brackets surrounding the discussion of the Ramsays and their guests have on your experience of reading "Time Passes"? What significance do you see in the fact that these characters' actions are bracketed off from the main narrative and Mrs. McNab's and Mrs. Bast's actions are not? (For biographical information about Virginia Woolf's relationships with her servants, see Light, especially 200–03, 216–19.)

CHAPTER 3

READING *TO THE LIGHTHOUSE*

Now is life very solid, or very shifting? I am haunted by the two contradictions. [. . .] Perhaps it may be that though we change; [. . .] we are somehow successive, & continuous—we human beings; & show the light through. But what is the light?
—*Virginia Woolf, 1929,* Diary *3*

Now, one may well ask oneself [. . .] how am I to read these books? What is the right way to set about it? [. . .] And is it pleasure, or profit, or what is it that I should seek? [. . .] I will make a few suggestions, which may serve to show you how not to read, or to stimulate you to think out better methods of your own.
—*Virginia Woolf, "How Should One Read a Book?," 1926,*
Essays *4*

"HOW SHOULD ONE READ A BOOK?"

I first read *To the Lighthouse* as an American exchange student at the University of Sussex in the mid-1980s. Being new to Woolf, I did not know then that the University's library is home to the Monks House Papers, a large archive of Virginia Woolf's letters and manuscripts—although I had read and enjoyed Vita Sackville-West's recently published correspondence to Woolf (1985). While there, during a break from studies, I set my sights on Sark, a small island off the south coast of England north of Brittany—the last feudal territory in Europe until its first democratic election in December 2008. Sark had been an artists' colony in the 1930s. Later, the Germans had used it as a base during World War II to launch their air attacks on the British mainland.

Upon landing at Creux Harbour, I was transported via tractor to La Malouine, a one-story stone bed and breakfast near the island's lighthouse, Point Robert Light. En route, golden licheny cliffs gave way to unmanicured gardens replete with roses, fuchsias, and hydrangeas. Soon the fog rolled in, and the foghorn echoed its alert. Except for the glow of stars and the occasional tractor and bicycle headlamp, all I could see from the guestroom window was the lighthouse's steady beam, stretching out to sea in two crisscrossed lines. It was in this setting that I first read *To the Lighthouse*. There was much about the novel that confounded me. Yet, the rhythm of the sentences and the watery atmosphere they created, as well as the imposing symbol of the lighthouse and Mr. Ramsay's imperious need for sympathy, fascinated me. The character of Lily Briscoe drew me in as well. I identified with the fact she had so many thoughts and opinions running through her mind all at once. And what did it mean for her to be described as having "Chinese eyes"? I wondered (17). Was Woolf using a racially offensive label to indicate that her female painter was in fact from China? At that time, I was a novice reader of Woolf. Having not yet considered pursuing a Ph.D. in English, let alone completed training as a literary scholar, I was also what Woolf referred to as a "common reader" (*Essays* 4: 19).

It may surprise the reader of this book, accustomed as we are to thinking about Virginia Woolf as an "important writer," to learn that she considered herself to be a "common reader" as well. What to make of this label? By "common reader" Woolf meant someone who was "not an academic" specialist in literature (Cuddy-Keane 69). And although Woolf wrote widely on books and authors and was sought out as a public intellectual, such as when she lectured to a girls' school (Hayes Court Common in Kent) on "How Should One Read a Book?" in January 1926 at the same time she was writing *To the Lighthouse*, she was not considered, nor did she consider herself to be, a professional scholar (Daughtery, "Virginia Woolf's" 123). Woolf envisioned the "common reader" as an inclusive category—any non-specialist who loved reading, particularly books that challenged conventional thinking. "Motivated by a desire for broad, inclusive knowledge and expanded human experience," the "common reader" read, but did not necessarily own, many books and approached them with an active mind, not desiring entertainment so much as intellectual engagement (Cuddy-Keane 117; see, also, 23–34, 59–114, 118, 128–29). For Woolf stimulating books owed their existence to intelligent, imaginative readers, and by this she did not mean professors of literature (V. Woolf, "How" [1932] 581–82; "Love" 273–74; "How" [Nov. 1925] 183–84 [MS 1.247]; Daugherty, "Virginia Woolf's" 130).

I begin this chapter with my recollections of first encountering *To the Lighthouse* and Woolf's thoughts about readers and reading in general because they highlight Woolf's and my shared cause with you, the reader of this book. Through years of teaching *To the Lighthouse* to undergraduates and graduate students in the United States, most coming to Woolf's writing for the first time, I have noticed a curious split: readers who take to the novel enthusiastically and those who feel a sense of, either singly or in combination, frustration, boredom, and alienation. I offer this information at the outset so that readers can measure their own responses to *To the Lighthouse* against mine and my students' and, perhaps, follow some of Woolf's advice to common readers.

Woolf revised her lecture "How Should One Read a Book?" and published three versions, one in October 1926 in the *Yale Review*, another in October 1932 in *The Second Common Reader*, and a shorter essay in 1931 re-titled "The Love of Reading" (Daugherty, "Virginia Woolf's" 123). In these essays, as well as in the different drafts of her lecture, Woolf elaborates on the responsibilities and value of common readers. On one hand, she acknowledges the hard work of reading: "To read a novel is a difficult and complex art. You must be capable not only of great fineness of perception, but of great boldness of imagination [. . .]" ("How" [1932] 575). On the other hand, she celebrates its pleasures, that "behind the erratic gunfire of the press [professional critics] [. . .] another kind of criticism, the opinion of people reading for the love of reading, slowly and unprofessionally, and judging with great sympathy and yet with great severity" can be heard ("How" [1932] 582).

Taken together, these pieces offer much savvy advice to readers (see Daugherty, "Virginia Woolf's" 131–32): One must trust one's "own instincts" and be an independent thinker ("How" [1926] 398; "How" [1932] 573). At the same time, the reader must not rush to judge a book until having read it in its entirety and having begun to reflect on it intensely ("How" [1926] 397, 398; "How" [1932] 573–74, 579–80). Discussing the book with others who have read it is encouraged

("How" [Nov. 1925] 182 [MS 1.243]). Checking one's own prejudices and preoccupations—about the author, the genre, the experiences described, the point of view—is essential ("How" [1926] 393; "How" [1932] 573; "Love" 272). The reader should not read submissively, bowing to the authority of others ("How" [1932] 573, 580). In particular, one should never rush to the critics for answers but instead develop for oneself an initial understanding of the novel before considering what critics have had to say ("How" [1926] 397; "Love" 273). According to Woolf, then, reading is not a passive activity ("How" [1926] 393). And nonprofessional readers can train themselves to become better readers by reading a lot of good literature, especially fiction, and contemplating it open-mindedly and critically ("How" [1932] 573, 581).

Woolf's musings provide an excellent entry into considering the reading process, linked as it is to larger critical debates about interpretation. Where does a book's meaning reside: within the author? the reader? the critic? the text? Or, as deconstructionists assert, is a text's meaning based on the nature of language itself? This chapter and the next will guide the reader through the process of interpreting *To the Lighthouse*, using multiple schema.

THE "WRITERLY TEXT"

As we saw in chapter 2 on Language, Style and Form, *To the Lighthouse* exemplifies what the French philosopher Roland Barthes referred to more generally in 1970 as a "writerly text" (in French, *scriptable*). By this Barthes meant a book that requires its reader to *make* it make sense by mentally filling in the gaps in language and narrative direction. He contrasts the "writerly text" to the "readerly text" (*lisible*) in which the reader is taken by the hand and shown how to make sense of the narrative by the straightforward language therein (*S/Z* 3–6). Barthes also declared "the death of the author." That is, he heralded the move away from interpretations based on deciphering "authorial intention" to those more concerned with the symbolic usage of language, what are referred to more broadly as "semiotic" or "deconstructionist" interpretations of literature (Barthes, "Death"; "From Work"). Following Barthes, literary critics no longer hold the author's intentions sacrosanct. An author's ideas about his or her work may be a useful place to begin one's interpretive process, as chapters 1 and 2 demonstrate, but they should not serve as the sole or even necessarily chief arbiter of the meaning of any given work.

Although Woolf asserts that the reader should be the writer's "accomplice" initially ("Love" 272), she suggests that the author's "preferences" as well as his or her "life" ultimately should not hold interpretive sway ("How" [1932] 576). And, like Barthes, Woolf emphasizes both the reader's and language's active role in the process of creating meaning. She contends, "a book is nothing like so solid as a building: words are more like fire than they are like clay. They change; they turn from green to blue. [. . .] They change from generation to generation. [. . .] [Y]ou [. . .] read [the same book] at a different angle from your grandmother. [. . .] You are seeing it with the light on the left side, & she with the light on the right side" ("How" [Nov. 1925] 147 [MS 1.191, 1.193]); see, also, Daugherty, "Virginia Woolf's" 127, 131).

This chapter as well as the entire guide is intended as a companion to *To the Lighthouse.* It is not meant to replace one's careful reading of the novel. It offers specific strategies and examples to enhance one's reading. Chapter 4 will provide an overview of the novel's reception history, including details about what literary critics over time have had to say. Ultimately, however, readers must develop their own opinions about what the book means. To paraphrase Woolf, see if you can "see the shape" of the novel ("How" [1932] 579) and "create for [your]self [. . .] some kind of whole" ("Common" 19).

PLOT, SETTING, AND CHARACTERS

As London music critic Neville Cardus wrote in 1932, "A man might as well hang himself as look for a story, a plot, in 'To the Lighthouse'" (11). His comments reflect the expectation of most readers approaching a novel for the first time, that is, that its storyline will engage them and be central to the reading experience. However, *To the Lighthouse* thwarts such readerly expectations. And although the novel concerns itself with character more so than with plot, here too it defies realist conventions. Arnold Bennett, a fellow writer always quick to criticize Woolf for what he saw as her failure at character development, faintly praised *To the Lighthouse* for the fact that "[h]er character drawing has improved. Mrs [sic] Ramsay almost amounts to a complete person" (200).

Despite the negligible plotting and the somewhat oblique character development, the story underpinning *To the Lighthouse* is fairly simple. It centers on two days, separated by ten years, in the life of the Ramsay family, their servants, and guests at their summer house on the Isle of Skye in the Inner Hebrides, small islands off the northwest coast of Scotland. The first and longest section of the novel, "The Window," takes place during "the middle of September" 1909 at "past six in the evening" (V. Woolf, *To the Lighthouse* 19; Lilienfeld, "Where" 149–50). Superficially, the narrative tension hinges on whether young James Ramsay will be able to sail to the lighthouse. Although disappointed at age six, he fulfills his desire at sixteen, accompanied by his sister Cam and his father, Mr. Ramsay. Simultaneously, Lily Briscoe, the unmarried middle-aged artist, completes her painting of Mrs. Ramsay after a ten-year hiatus. The narrative climax of the first 160 pages ("The Window" section) is Mrs. Ramsay's dinner party, during which a marriage proposal is announced, artistic problems are resolved, and much soup and Bœuf en Daube are consumed.

The middle section of the novel, "Time Passes," shifts the narrative focus from characters and family life to the elements of nature and the life of a nation engaged in its first world war. The novel's central character, Mrs. Ramsay, dies, as do two of her children, Andrew, in wartime battle, and Prue, after giving birth. Their abandoned summer house languishes in disrepair only to be resuscitated years later by Mrs. McNab and Mrs. Bast, two industrious elderly women hired to prepare it for the family's return in the final section ("The Lighthouse").

THE METAPHYSICS OF THE NOVEL

The first epigraph to this chapter, a passage from Woolf's diary, represents the philosophical axis upon which *To the Lighthouse* revolves. The novel asks the question, Are human character and human life enduring or fleeting? If fleeting, What is the point to life? When considered from a perspective wider than a single human life, What is the purpose of human beings' elaborate rituals—our attempts to communicate with each other, through personal interaction and the creation of art, and our fight to the death battles, both filial and military? The intricacies of *To the Lighthouse*—its method of character development, the stream-of-consciousness style, the prominent imagery of waves, lighthouse, and horizon, the organization into three uneven sections representing extremes of time before and after

World War I, and the focus on childhood and memory—combine to underscore a central paradox: life is at once eternal and momentary, made up of opposing forces of stasis and flow.

Despite this singular epistemological underpinning, *To the Lighthouse* can be interpreted in myriad ways, to which more than eight decades of review and literary criticism attest. In what follows, I will discuss four sometimes overlapping interpretive schemas for understanding the novel: "Marriage of Opposites," "A Portrait of the Artist as a Middle-Aged Woman," "Unclassified Affections," and "Political Silences." Within each schema, many different readings are possible, and I will provide examples of how particular passages work individually and in concert to establish several contrasting yet similarly legitimate interpretations of the novel.

"Marriage of Opposites"

In her essay *A Room of One's Own*, Woolf asserts that in order to write well one must write from a gender-neutral place by cultivating an "androgynous mind" (98). Without mental androgyny, Woolf argues, its opposite, sex consciousness, tends to overwhelm the writer's mind, often leading to literature that praises one sex over the other or denounces the injustices perpetuated in the name of sex differences. Permeated with arrogance or anger, such literature fails to achieve a writer's aesthetic vision. Woolf uses the metaphor of fertilization through heterosexual union to argue her point: that "[s]ome collaboration has to take place in the [individual writer's] mind between the woman and the man before the act of creation can be accomplished. Some marriage of opposites has to be consummated" (104).

This idea of the "marriage of opposites" provides a useful metaphor for interpreting *To the Lighthouse*, published one year prior to Woolf's lectures that would become *A Room of One's Own*. Which opposites command one's attention and what they mean in the context of the novel provoke diverse responses, however (see, for example, Briggs, *Virginia Woolf* 163; Banfield, *Phantom* 145, 148–54). Other critics, most notably Gayatri Spivak, reject the androgyny schema as too simplistic, even a misreading of the novel (40, 42, 43). Must one approach the "marriage of opposites" literally and so interpret *To the Lighthouse* as centrally concerned with the vicissitudes of heterosexual union? May one also understand masculinity and femininity to be abstractions, social not biological imperatives, as Woolf suggests in *A Room of One's Own*? If so, perhaps the novel has something to say about the need to merge gender identities within the individual and society in order to attain an androgynous ideal. Does the novel offer a more pointed feminist critique of the insufficiencies, even dangers, of unchecked masculinity, which is characteristic of patriarchal societies? Along these lines, must the qualities of rationalism and empiricism be tempered by ethical, humanistic, and aesthetic concerns in order to promote the common good? One might substitute such social and political attributes with temporal and historical ones to conclude that *To the Lighthouse* forces an unholy marriage between the Victorian ethos and the modern Zeitgeist. Or, perhaps the novel pertains to conflicting ways of perceiving the universe: for example, what one assumes constitutes another person versus what that person experiences him- or herself to be.

Let us begin by examining the literal interpretation of the "marriage of opposites," the couple at the center of *To the Lighthouse*, Mr. and Mrs. Ramsay. Modeled after Woolf's parents, Leslie and Julia Stephen, they represent if not opposites then at least divergent temperaments and epistemologies (see Derbyshire; J. Bennett; Brogan; H. Russell). In the novel's complex elongated opening scene, which begins *in medias res* and extends for sixty-two pages, three sets of characters are engaged in simultaneous conversations: Mrs. Ramsay with her young son James; Mr. Ramsay with his philosophy mentee Charles Tansley; and Lily Briscoe with William Bankes. Ensconced with James, who is sitting on the floor beside her, Mrs. Ramsay is knitting a stocking for the lighthouse keeper's son while posing for Lily's painting. Later she reads to James the Grimms' fairy tale "The Fisherman and His Wife" until the servant Mildred carries him out of the room. Concurrently, on the terrace, just outside the open window that frames mother and child, Mr. Ramsay and Tansley are pacing while discussing philosophy, occasionally interjecting comments into Mrs. Ramsay and James's conversation. Simultaneously, Lily, whose easel is set up outside on the edge of the lawn, is attempting to paint a portrait of Mrs. Ramsay while Mr. Ramsay's friend William Bankes, a widowed botanist, looks on, engaging her in conversation. Focused on Mr. and Mrs. Ramsay's differing responses to their son's question about whether the voyage to the lighthouse will take place, the passage below, which has been heavily condensed, illustrates some crucial contrasts between husband and wife:

> "Yes, of course, if it's fine tomorrow," said Mrs. Ramsay. "But you'll have to be up with the lark," she added.[. . .]
>
> "But," said his [James's] father, stopping in front of the drawing-room window, "it won't be fine."[. . .]
>
> "Perhaps you will wake up and find the sun shining and the birds singing," she said compassionately, soothing the little boy's hair, for her husband, with his caustic saying that it would not be fine, had dashed his spirits she could see. [. . .]
>
> "And even if it isn't fine tomorrow," said Mrs. Ramsay, [. . .] "it will be another day." [. . .] She stroked James's head; she transferred to him what she felt for her husband, and, as she watched him chalk yellow the white dress shirt of a gentleman in the Army and Navy Stores catalogue, thought what a delight it would be to her should he turn out a great artist; and why should he not? [. . .] Then, looking up, as her husband passed her once more, she was relieved to find that the ruin was veiled; domesticity triumphed; custom crooned its soothing rhythm, so that when stopping deliberately, as his turn came round again, at the window he bent quizzically and whimsically to tickle James's bare calf with a sprig of something, she twitted him for having dispatched "that poor young man," Charles Tansley. Tansley had had to go in and write his dissertation, he said.
>
> "James will have to write *his* dissertation one of these days," he added ironically. [. . .]
>
> There wasn't the slightest possible chance that they could go to the Lighthouse tomorrow, Mr. Ramsay snapped out irascibly.
>
> How did he know? she asked. The wind often changed.
>
> The extraordinary irrationality of her remark, the folly of women's minds enraged him. [. . .] [S]he flew in the face of facts, made his children hope what was utterly out of the question, in effect, told lies. He stamped his foot on the stone step. "Damn you," he said. But what had she said? Simply that it might be fine tomorrow. So it might.
>
> Not with the barometer falling and the wind due west.
>
> To pursue truth with such astonishing lack of consideration for other people's feelings, to rend the thin veils of civilisation so wantonly, so brutally, was to her so horrible an outrage of human

decency that, without replying, dazed and blinded, she bent her head. [. . .] There was nothing to be said.

He stood by her in silence. Very humbly, at length, he said that he would step over and ask the Coastguards if she liked.

There was nobody whom she reverenced as she reverenced him. (3, 4, 15, 26, 31–32)

Seemingly a mere disagreement about the weather, this marital squabble betrays fundamental differences between Mr. and Mrs. Ramsay that spark dissension in their union. Mr. Ramsay uses objective data gleaned from direct observation and scientific instruments—in this situation, "the barometer falling and the wind due west" (32)—to support his views without considering their effects on actual human beings. His devotion to pursuing the unadorned truth at any cost, or as Lily imagines of his particular philosophical approach—"this seeing of angular essences, this reducing of lovely evenings, with all their flamingo clouds and blue and silver to a white deal [softwood] four-legged table" (23)—dictates his approach to human interactions in general.

By contrast, Mrs. Ramsay elevates the importance of people's feelings over other considerations. Her interactions are guided by a fine-tuned sense of individual human needs as well as the understanding that multiple truths coexist and communal harmony requires self-sacrifice. Thus, she finds abhorrent her husband's seemingly callous behavior, just as he recoils from her apparent irrationality. She delights in imagining James an artist; he, in his self-centeredness, assumes his son will become an academic like himself. (For an alternative interpretation of this scene, see Doyle, "These Emotions" 50–52; "Voyaging" 151, 160, 163–65.)

It is tempting, though ill-advised, to read Mr. and Mrs. Ramsay's differences as confirming an essential gender dichotomy—that men are guided by fact and reason; women, by emotion and the demands of family and custom. In fact, Mr. Ramsay believes such a notion to be fact when he declares here and elsewhere in the novel "the folly of women's minds" (31). Such an interpretation falls short, however, because it fails to account for the inherent contradictions within each character (see Lilienfeld, "Deceptiveness"). Mr. Ramsay, who in the passage above stomps his foot like an ill-behaved child and swears at his wife when she challenges his views, is hardly a model of dispassion and sagacity. Furthermore, though he claims to care only for the scientific truth and appears oblivious to others' feelings, he becomes so engrossed in the beauty of literature—particularly, for the emotions it invokes in him through identification—that he loses all sense of equilibrium. As he recites lines from "The Charge of the Light Brigade," the famous lyric recounting the slaughter of over one hundred British soldiers during a battle of the Crimean War, he loses his composure and literally charges into Lily Briscoe and William Bankes:

> His eyes, glazed with emotion, defiant with tragic intensity, met theirs. [. . .] [H]e impressed upon them his own child-like resentment of interruption, yet even in the moment of discovery was not to be routed utterly, but was determined to hold fast to something of this delicious emotion, this impure rhapsody of which he was ashamed, but in which he revelled—[. . .]
>
> He shivered; he quivered. All his vanity, all his satisfaction in his own splendour, [. . .] had been shattered, destroyed. Stormed at by shot and shell, boldly we rode and well, flashed through the valley of death, volleyed and thundered—straight into Lily Briscoe and William Bankes. He quivered; he shivered. (25, 30)

Mr. Ramsay feels shame for experiencing "this delicious emotion" and for being observed during the height of emotional ecstasy. Later in the day, while reading Sir Walter Scott's novel *The Antiquary*, "he felt roused and triumphant and could not choke back his tears. Raising the book a little to hide his face, he let them fall and shook his head from side to side and forgot himself completely [. . .]" (120). Mr. Ramsay may cast himself as the dispassionate rationalist or the stoic commander who soldiers on (see Baldanza; McVicker, "Reading"; Phillips; Doyle, "Voyaging"); however, his overweening emotional response to Tennyson and Scott and his desperate need for women's sympathy demonstrated elsewhere in the novel betray the insufficiency of his internalized gender stereotypes.

For her part, Mrs. Ramsay displays her own brand of inconstancy. Her judgments of people and relationships change often and abruptly. In the long passage above, for example, she considers her husband to be "uncivilized" one moment and almost Godlike the next. She continually extols the institution of marriage, believing that "an unmarried woman has missed the best of life" (49), yet also wonders secretly, "But what have I done with my life?" (82). In the evening at the dinner table, her perception of her husband continues to vacillate: "[s]he could not understand how she had ever felt any emotion or affection for him" (83), and then a few moments later "she admired him so much" that she "glowed all over" (95). His "scowling and frowning, and flushing with anger" (95) over his friend, the poet and translator, Augustus Carmichael's request for more soup vexes her; but his predictable attraction to "Minta's glow" transforms him again, in Mrs. Ramsay's eyes, into a "gallant" man "with delightful ways" who "looked astonishingly young" (99).

Despite their contrarieties, Mr. and Mrs. Ramsay manage to create moments of equilibrium as a married couple. As we saw in the passage above about visiting the lighthouse, Mrs. Ramsay relies on the "soothing rhythm" (31) of familial customs to lull discord and suspend chaos. Mr. Ramsay instead looks to epic themes of battle, duty, and chivalry to transform his anger over women's "irrationality" (31) into striving for "success in love" (Karras 25).

Rather than reducing Mr. and Mrs. Ramsay to masculine and feminine archetypes, then, we might interpret the couple as representing opposing epistemological frameworks (see Henke). The lens through which Mr. Ramsay views the world filters data conceptually based on broad abstractions. His model for organizing information is the epic poem, such as Tennyson's "The Charge of the Light Brigade," in which grand-scale global conflict, duty for one's country, and heroic death in battle are mythologized in a tightly organized, well-established verse form (Phillips; Goldman, *Feminist*; S. Friedman).

By contrast, Mrs. Ramsay's lens focuses on the quotidian and the material, the fleeting and the marginal, and thus the seemingly insignificant: the momentary beauty of flowers and joys of a summer's evening stroll, the immediate needs of a child or a sick widow in distress, human beings ridiculed or lives carried on in obscurity. Mrs. Ramsay's distress over her children's attacks on Charles Tansley's character becomes a larger commentary on the perils of "inventing differences, when people, [. . .] were different enough. [. . .] She had in mind at the moment, rich and poor, high and low; [. . .] and the things she saw with her own eyes, weekly, daily, here or in London, when she visited this widow, or that struggling wife in person with a bag on her arm [. . .]" (8–9). Mrs. Ramsay not only bears witness to human suffering in her midst but also takes pains to ameliorate it—whereas Mr. Ramsay, although moved to tears by artistic accounts of human struggle in an epic poem and a well-wrought novel, tries to filter out from view its more mundane forms.

Mrs. Ramsay's focus on domestic life—in all its minutiae and impermanency—enables her to see the fluidity of human character. Take, for example, her response to Charles Tansley. At the dinner party, the same scene in which her husband appears at once galling and gallant, Mrs. Ramsay finds Tansley to be an utter egotist, always "want[ing] to assert himself [. . .] saying, 'I-I-I'" (106); yet, at the same time, she pities him (84–85, 104). Later, in "The Lighthouse" section, we learn that Mrs. Ramsay's capacious storehouse of sympathy enabled her, and eventually Lily, to see Tansley as someone who was "as nice as he could possibly be" (160; see Henke). In other words, Mrs. Ramsay's capacity to detect and succor people's vulnerabilities as well as hold in balance life's contradictions gives her extraordinary powers for good (see Lilienfeld, "Deceptiveness"). According to Lily, this strength also makes Mrs. Ramsay an artist of sorts. Just as Lily reduces the myriad elements of daily life to a few abstract shapes and colors on her canvas, concerned as she is with "the relations of masses" (53) and "the unity of the whole" (53), Mrs. Ramsay

> brought together this and that and then this, and so made out of that miserable silliness and spite [. . .] something—[. . .] which survived, [. . .] affecting one almost like a work of art. [. . .] Mrs. Ramsay bringing them together; Mrs. Ramsay saying, "Life stand still here"; Mrs. Ramsay making of the moment something permanent (as in another sphere Lily herself tried to make of the moment something permanent)—. [. . .] In the midst of chaos there was shape; this eternal passing and flowing [. . .] was struck into stability. (160, 161)

From Lily's perspective, Mrs. Ramsay is her artistic counterpart: a Victorian wife and mother whose paints are life's moments, "eternal[ly] passing and flowing" (161), and whose canvas is the domestic sphere.

Because *To the Lighthouse* links Lily and Mrs. Ramsay—one is an artist literally and the other metaphorically—and in general brings together characters who straddle two different centuries, several critics have interpreted the "marriage of opposites" theme to mean the bridging of eras and ethoses: specifically, the Victorian and the modern (see, for example, Briggs, *Virginia Woolf* 171, 174–76). If *To the Lighthouse* illustrates the difficult merging of Victorian and modern values, then Mrs. Ramsay represents the Victorian "angel in the house," whose duty is to minister to others' needs (Phillips 96–98, 232; see, also, Doyle, "Voyaging" 143); Lily stands for the modern or "New Woman," a turn-of-the-century icon personified by such fashion and technological inventions as bloomers and the bicycle and ushered in by the fight for women's rights. As the reforms sought by Victorian feminists began to be realized in the twentieth century, and women became less economically dependent upon men, middle-class women could choose a profession other than marriage and motherhood as their life's work.

The historical phenomenon of middle-class women's broadening opportunities in the early twentieth century, epitomized by the "New Woman," gives force to Lily's internal dialogue at the dinner party: "she need not marry, thank Heaven: she need not undergo that degradation. She was saved from that dilution. She would move the tree rather more to the middle" (102). Put simply, because Lily renounces marriage, she has the freedom to develop her own talents rather than, as is the case for Mrs. Ramsay, those of a husband and children. Lily's musing, in the passage above, about "mov[ing] the tree rather more to the middle" becomes shorthand for her determination to continue painting. It is her life's work, which "she would always go on" doing not because she had to but simply "because it interested her" (72). Lily's alternate vision of womanhood to Mrs. Ramsay's represents more broadly, then, the modern woman's rejection of middle-class Victorian mores, particularly the imperative to marry and bear children (see Emery; Phillips; Froula; Doyle, "Voyaging").

Despite Lily's eschewing marriage, however, she remains ambivalent about heterosexual romantic love, particularly as she witnesses the aura of enchantment enveloping a newly engaged couple, the Ramsays' young guests, Minta Doyle and Paul Rayley.

[W]hat happened to her, especially staying with the Ramsays, was to be made to feel violently two opposite things at the same time; that's what you feel, was one; that's what I feel, was the other, and then they fought together in her mind, as now. It is so beautiful, so exciting, this love, that I tremble on the verge of it, and offer, quite out of my own habit, to look for a brooch on a beach; also it is the stupidest, the most barbaric of human passions, and turns a nice young man with a profile like a gem's (Paul's was exquisite) into a

bully with a crowbar (he was swaggering, he was insolent). [. . .]
Yet, she said to herself, from the dawn of time odes have been sung
to love; wreaths heaped and roses; and if you asked nine people
out of ten they would say they wanted nothing but this—love;
while the women, judging from her own experience, would all the
time be feeling, This is not what we want; there is nothing more
tedious, puerile, and inhumane than this; yet it is also beautiful
and necessary. (102–03)

Here, as throughout the dinner party scene, the novel offers one of its
sharpest critiques of the institution of marriage, especially its rein-
forcement of male privilege. Filtered through Lily's perspective, the
passage, in effect, says that society leads a young man to believe that
playing at being chivalrous so as to woo a young woman into marriage confirms his masculine prerogative, thereby turning him into
"a bully with a crowbar." Implied elsewhere in the novel, in lines such
as "an unmarried woman has missed the best of life" (49), society
leads a young woman to believe that joining herself to a man in
marriage is her destiny and only means of fulfillment. (For another
interpretation of this scene, see Briggs, *Virginia Woolf* 172.)

The "marriage of opposites" theme is here turned inside out.
Mrs. Ramsay and Lily are the "opposites of marriage"; that is, their
views on marriage are in opposition, yet each also feels momentarily
in conflict with herself about the institution. For example, Mrs.
Ramsay finds both happiness and discontentment within her own
marriage, yet nonetheless feels compelled to "le[ad] her victims [. . .]
to the altar" (101). Lily recoils from the social imperative to marry,
yet longs for the adventure and intimacy implied by Paul and Minta's
betrothal, which emanates "the emotion, the vibration, of love" (101;
see Briggs, *Virginia Woolf* 171).

Unlike Lily and Mrs. Ramsay, who despite their differing historical vantage points share a mutual respect for what each has made of
her life choices, Woolf viewed the gulf between her desires and those
her elders had for her to be unbridgeable. In her unfinished memoir,
"A Sketch of the Past," she describes the years after her mother's
death during which the values and conventions of two opposing eras
dictated the Stephen sisters' bifurcated lives. In the late morning she
and her sister were allowed to cultivate their artistic and intellectual
talents undisturbed by social proprieties and responsibilities. By late
afternoon, however, they had to dress for tea and greet guests to the

Stephen home and later, repeat the routine for evening parties. As referred to in chapter 1, Virginia Stephen was made to feel as if she were a prized horse on display. From Woolf's perspective, then, the Victorian and modern eras were not so much marrying during the author's adolescence as they were colliding. The Stephen women embraced the modern age and envisioned the future, and the Duckworth men (the sisters' step-brothers) attempted to restrain them by confining them to the past. As Woolf recalled: "Explorers and revolutionists, as we both were by nature, we lived under the sway of a society that was about fifty years too old for us. [. . .] We were living say in 1910; they [Leslie Stephen, and George and Gerald Duckworth] were living in 1860" ("Sketch" 147).

Portrait of the Artist as a Middle-Aged Woman

This idea of the Stephen sisters as "[e]xplorers and revolutionists," as modern women creating new ways to approach art and life in contradiction to the rules imposed by their elders, points to a second schema for interpreting *To the Lighthouse*, the *Künstlerroman* ("artist's novel") (Emery; Goldman, *Feminist*; Briggs, *Virginia Woolf* 179–80). Like James Joyce's 1916 *A Portrait of the Artist as a Young Man*, Woolf's 1927 novel focuses on the development of the artist. Unlike Joyce's protagonist, Stephen Dedalus, however, Woolf's Lily Briscoe is middle-aged and female—thirty-three when the novel opens in an era when an unmarried woman of twenty-five was considered a "spinster." Interpretations of *To the Lighthouse* that focus on the figure of the female artist often explore biographical connections between Lily Briscoe and either Vanessa Bell or Virginia Woolf (see, for example, Froula). These readings are concerned with what the novel has to say about aesthetics and the art world: what artistic values and dilemmas avant-gardism embraced in the wake of nineteenth-century realism and what challenges women artists faced in traditionally masculine-controlled domains. More abstractly, this schema opens up meta-textual readings in which Lily's painting serves as a metaphor for the novel itself.

A year after publishing *To the Lighthouse,* in her lectures that would become *A Room of One's Own*, Woolf would explore in detail the obstacles women writers have faced historically, such as the lack of a female literary tradition and uninterrupted time. In *To the Lighthouse* we catch glimpses of one such obstacle, society's attitudes toward women generally, and female artists particularly. Mr. Ramsay's dismissal of "the folly of women's minds" (31) and Charles Tansley's chant "'Women can't paint, women can't write . . .'" (48) give voice to society's chauvinism, which undermines the female artist's confidence in herself. According to Diane Filby Gillespie in *The Sisters' Arts: The Writing and Painting of Virginia Woolf and Vanessa Bell*, "both sisters, like Lily Briscoe in *To the Lighthouse*, struggled to assert their own views and needs in the face of traditional domestic pressures and artistic theories . . ." (11). Like Vanessa Stephen, who, in the midst of developing her craft, managed the Stephen household after the deaths of her mother and stepsister (Spalding 24–25), Lily Briscoe balances the demands of her art with caring for her father (19).

Early in the novel, we get our first glimpse of Lily through the eyes of Mrs. Ramsay. She expresses relief that it is "[o]nly Lily Briscoe" who falls victim to her husband's self-absorption, his bellowing of Tennyson and near collision with Lily's easel (17). "[S]tanding on the edge of the lawn painting," Lily is positioned on the periphery of the Ramsays' house, the novel's main setting, as if to suggest her outsider status (17). "With her little Chinese eyes and her puckered-up face, she would never marry; one could not take her painting very seriously [. . .]" (17). This description suggests Lily's unimportance, even aberrance. Vanessa Bell, who thought *To the Lighthouse* "bewitch[ing]" for its uncanny incarnation of her mother, wanted confirmation from her sister that "surely Lily Briscoe must have been rather a good painter—before her time perhaps, but with great gifts really?" (V. Woolf, *Letters* 3: 574, 573). Even Lily questions her gifts as a painter. "It would be hung in the attics, she thought; it would be destroyed" (208). She is filled with self-doubt throughout the story until the novel's last line.

Despite this lack of confidence, Lily triumphs in that she sees her painting of Mrs. Ramsay—after a ten-year interruption, three deaths, and a world war—through to its completion. "But what did that matter? she asked herself, taking up her brush again. [. . .] With a sudden intensity, as if she saw it clear for a second, she drew a line there, in the centre. It was done; it was finished. Yes, she thought, laying down her brush in extreme fatigue, I have had my vision" (208, 209). Lily's determination to have her "vision"—despite being told, "[w]omen can't paint" (48), despite fearing her painting "would be destroyed" (208)—solidifies her commitment to her own painterly process.

She continues to create art and to believe in the importance of art even in the midst of life's chaos and impermanency.

What does it mean that Lily has "little Chinese eyes"? This detail both disturbs and confounds. Should we dismiss the descriptor as irrelevant except as a trace of the racial prejudices we find more pronounced elsewhere within Woolf's writings, such as in her *Diary* and the novels *Orlando* (1928) and *The Years* (1937)? Perhaps Lily's being marked as "racially other" merely underscores her outsider status along gendered lines (Abel, "Matrilineage"; Doyle, "Voyaging"). After all, she is a middle-aged, middle-class Englishwoman who refuses to marry and bear children. Some critics take this feminist analysis further to equate Lily's gender transgressions with resistance to imperialist norms as well. Lily's marriage resistance, they argue, signifies her rejection of any institution bound up with patriarchy, particularly patriotism, imperialism, and white supremacy (Phillips; Winston), topics to which I will return. Another interpretation, from Patricia Laurence in her book *Lily Briscoe's Chinese Eyes: Bloomsbury, Modernism and China* (2003), speaks to Lily's artistic influences. According to Laurence, Lily, like many modernist painters of her day, including Vanessa Bell and Roger Fry, looks to Asia, particularly China, for aesthetic inspiration, transposing Chinese painterly techniques and philosophy to an English modernist context (210, 240–41, 326, 346, 351, 387). (For discussion of Lily's "Chinese eyes," see, also, Seshagiri; Hayot.)

Mrs. Ramsay's description of Lily's "little Chinese eyes and her puckered-up face" (17) followed by the remark that she would never marry, suggests Lily is physically unattractive, at least according to conventional European standards of feminine beauty (Auerbach; Emery). This is another contrast between her and Mrs. Ramsay, who, as was true of Julia Prinsep Stephen, is renowned for her beauty. Together these interpretations support the conclusion that Lily not only looks but also sees differently from others. As a painter, and an experimental modernist one at that, her eyes perceive the world differently, and she transforms those perceptions into something unconventional in her art (Abel, "Matrilineage").

That Lily is a Post-Impressionist painter—instead of the "sentimental Sunday painter" that Woolf initially envisioned (Briggs, *Virginia Woolf* 166)—is implied by the glimpses we catch of her canvas. Although vague, the descriptions of her painting serve to ally her with Vanessa Bell's abstract paintings and riotous use of color

(Gillespie, *Sisters'*; Goldman, *Feminist*; Tickner) and the aesthetics advocated by Roger Fry and by Clive Bell, whose idea of "significant form" privileges a painting's inherent formal dimensions over symbolism and fidelity to nature (Roberts, "Vision"): "she scored her canvas with brown running nervous lines which had no sooner settled there than they enclosed (she felt it looming out at her) a space" (158). That is, Lily is centrally concerned with her painting's formal properties—"the relations of masses, of lights and shadows" (53)— and bold use of color rather than any "attempt at likeness" (52) of a real-life subject.

Her non-mimetic style bewilders the widowed botanist, William Bankes. His tastes conform to conventional standards of beauty. Thus, he admires Mrs. Ramsay for her feminine good looks and appreciates representational art, including the "cherry trees in blossom on the banks of the Kennet" (53) and the great masters' classical renderings of the human form:

> What did she wish to indicate by the triangular purple shape, "just there"? he asked.
>
> It was Mrs. Ramsay reading to James, she said. She knew his objection—that no one could tell it for a human shape. But she had made no attempt at likeness, she said. For what reason had she introduced them then? he asked. Why indeed?—except that if there, in that corner, it was bright, here, in this, she felt the need of darkness. [. . .] Mother and child then—objects of universal veneration, and in this case the mother was famous for her beauty—might be reduced, he pondered, to a purple shadow without irreverence.
>
> But the picture was not of them, she said. Or, not in his sense. There were other senses too in which one might reverence them. By a shadow here and a light there, for instance. (52)

Incomprehensible to William Bankes, "the triangular purple shape" that represents Mrs. Ramsay on Lily's canvas resembles the "august shape [. . .] of a dome" (52, 51) that Lily imagines, after a shared moment of intimacy, symbolizes her friend's essential core. Significantly, Lily's vision of Mrs. Ramsay matches the "wedge-shaped core of darkness" Mrs. Ramsay knows her private self to be (62; see Roberts, "Vision"). Lily uses her trained artist's eyes as well as her reverence for Mrs. Ramsay's beauty—that is, Mrs. Ramsay's uniqueness as a woman rather than her conformity to standards of feminine grace—to capture "the essential thing" (49) about her, the seemingly elusive spirit of Mrs. Ramsay.

Even if her painting "would be rolled up and flung under a sofa," Lily concludes that "what it attempted," that is, to give form to the essence of Mrs. Ramsay, whom she loves, "'remained for ever'" (179). What matters, then, is the artist's ongoing struggle to impose order on the transient and seemingly disparate elements of life, and thereby represent something of life's beauty and intensity. As discussed above, Mrs. Ramsay orchestrates an elaborate ritual carried out at the dinner table so that the ordinary pettiness of human intercourse and the disparate elements of daily life are transformed into something remarkable. In attempting to capture Mrs. Ramsay in art, to see past pretense, convention, and even physical beauty to a numinous inner quality, Lily, too, tries to create meaning out of chaos. (For an alternative conceptual framing of Lily's attempts to capture Mrs. Ramsay in art, see Spivak, especially 30–31, 43.)

Because of its focus on the artist, the *Künstlerroman* schema invites meta-textual analysis as well—identifying passages in which the novel appears to comment on *itself* as a constructed literary work and on the function of art in society more generally. Take, for example, the passage in the sailboat in which Cam describes her father's reading habits: "He read [. . .] as if he were guiding something, or wheedling a large flock of sheep, or pushing his way up and up a single narrow path; and sometimes he went fast and straight, and broke his way through the bramble, and sometimes it seemed a branch struck at him, a bramble blinded him, but he was not going to let himself be beaten by that [. . .]" (190). This passage might aptly describe the reader of *To the Lighthouse* as well. Perhaps one has felt struck by a branch or blinded by a bramble while trying to decipher the meaning of a particular scene.

Other meta-textual moments in *To the Lighthouse* engage aesthetic concerns central to modernism. "Time Passes" offers several examples. As discussed in chapter 2, "Time Passes" experiments with the passage of time, condensing a ten-year stretch into twenty pages and bracketing off the deaths of significant characters into parenthetical asides. (For discussion of "Time Passes," see Derbyshire; Flint; Spivak; Haule, "*To the Lighthouse*"; Doyle, "Voyaging"; Emery; Levenback; Sherman.) Yet this section also addresses some of the most probing aesthetic questions raised in the novel. Is it possible to create art in an age of world war? And if one continues to pursue aesthetic aims, how will such catastrophic destruction affect one's finished creations and the very notion of beauty?

The novel approaches these questions obliquely in chapters 5 and 6 of "Time Passes," which lead up to the beginning of World War I. With the exception of Mrs. McNab and Mrs. Bast, the working-class women hired to clean the summer house, and Mrs. Bast's son George (see chapter 4 for discussion of Mrs. McNab), and the brief mention of Mrs. Ramsay's, Prue Ramsay's, and Andrew Ramsay's deaths, human life in these chapters exists as a disembodied collective, "those who had gone down to pace the beach" (133). That this collective represents society's artists is suggested by the fact that it contains "[t]he mystic, the visionary," persons who seek answers to such essential questions as, "'What am I,' 'What is this?'" (131). Before the War begins, they are "hopeful" that the wonder of the natural world will reassure them that "good triumphs, happiness prevails, order rules," or, at least, that the beauty of art will make them feel "secure" (132). Once World War I commences, however, they cannot ignore the "ominous sounds" of "agony" or the "purplish stain" on the sea, indicating that there was now "something out of harmony" (133):

> There was the silent apparition of an ashen-coloured ship for instance, come, gone; there was a purplish stain upon the bland surface of the sea as if something had boiled and bled, invisibly, beneath. This intrusion into a scene calculated to stir the most sublime reflections and lead to the most comfortable conclusions stayed their pacing. It was difficult blandly to overlook them; to abolish their significance in the landscape. (133–34)

Here, Woolf appears to be questioning how the artist can go on creating art as she did before, now that the Great War has changed life completely (Winston). At the end of the chapter, we learn that "to pace the beach was impossible; contemplation [of the relation between man and Nature] was unendurable; the mirror was broken" (134). In other words, art that holds the mirror up to nature is no longer tenable in an age of world war (Levenback 106–13; Briggs, *Virginia Woolf* 176). (For alternative interpretations, see Caughie, "How" 272; Doyle, "These Emotions" 62; "Voyaging" 165–66.) Ordinary people, who eagerly embrace Augustus Carmichael's latest book of poetry, desire something conventional to soothe them in a time of desolation (134). According to Woolf, however, "poetry [. . .]

is a hobbled, shackled tongue tied vehicle [. . .] for the voice of the soul [. . .] speaks in prose" (*Letters* 3: 359). The artist believes a new prose must be born.

Extending this meta-textual interpretation further, several critics view Lily's painting as an analogue for Woolf's novel *To the Lighthouse* (Beach; Roberts, "Vision"; Doyle, "Voyaging"). "Beautiful and bright it should be on the surface, feathery and evanescent, one colour melting into another like the colours of a butterfly's wing; but beneath the fabric must be clamped together with bolts of iron" (*To the Lighthouse* 171). In other words, Lily's approach to painting reflects Woolf's techniques in novel writing. Like Lily, who paints Mrs. Ramsay as a purple triangular shape unrecognizable as a human form, Woolf attempts to manifest in words the essence of her parents, Julia and Leslie Stephen, without writing a biography in the realist style that recounts their lives. Lily's "bolts of iron" beneath the shimmering surface of color refer to the rigorous technique she, as did Woolf, employs to create the effect of ease and transparency on her canvas. Lily recalls, ten years after her first attempt to paint Mrs. Ramsay, that "[t]here had been a problem about a foreground of a picture," and she had had a "revelation" at the dinner table about how to solve it (147). "The question was of some relation between those masses" (147–48). Both painting and writing involve intellectual challenges, aesthetic problems, and political complexities that, if solved successfully, do not mar the beautiful surface of the finished piece. Woolf was satisfied she had successfully achieved the stylistic experiment in language she had launched in *To the Lighthouse*. "[H]ow lovely some parts of The Lighthouse are! Soft & pliable, & I think deep, & never a word wrong for a page at a time" (*Diary* 3: 132). She especially admired the dinner party scene and Cam and James sailing to the lighthouse but, except for the ending, was not entirely pleased with the passages about Lily painting.

Interestingly, Lily's moment of revelation, in which she realizes how to paint her elusive subject after a ten-year hiatus, involves an experience with words similar to one Mrs. Ramsay has had ten years earlier. In "The Window" section, directly after the dinner party, Mrs. Ramsay hears Charles Elton's "Luriana, Lurilee" resound in her head to the point that the poem's "words, like little shaded lights, one red, one blue, one yellow, lit up in the dark of her mind, and seemed leaving their perches up there to fly across and across, or to cry out and to be echoed [. . .]" (119). In "The Lighthouse" section, in which Lily returns to the Ramsays a decade later, she remembers the lines from William Cowper's "The Castaway" that Mr. Ramsay often recited. So intense is her recollection that "the words became symbols, wrote themselves all over the grey-green walls" of the dining room (147). In response to hearing poetry, both women perceive words anew, unmoored from their conventional meanings. These moments in the novel where words seem to break free of syntax and semantics to become colors, pure sounds, and icons reflect Woolf's desire, as she set out to write *To the Lighthouse*, to "[c]atch them [thoughts] hot & sudden as they rise in the mind [. . .]" (*Diary* 3: 102), to capture "the thing itself before its [sic] made into anything: the emotion, the idea" (*Letters* 3: 321) unmediated by the rules and properties of language.

Other moments of revelation, "moments of being" Woolf called them, connect Lily's perceptions and way of thinking to Mrs. Ramsay's. These moments are private in that each character experiences them inwardly, yet parallel in that similar characteristics distinguish them. During these moments, which appear to be engendered by the women's creative capacities, quotidian concerns fall away to reveal a broader perspective on life. Intense delight floods the mind, and energy seems to radiate throughout the body.

Mrs. Ramsay experiences her "moments of being" in the midst of reading to James and knitting a stocking for the lighthouse keeper's son, until her husband interrupts her reverie to demand sympathy (37). Mrs. Ramsay suddenly appears to metamorphose:

> to pour erect into the air a rain of energy, a column of spray, looking at the same time animated and alive as if all her energies were being fused into force, burning and illuminating [. . .] and into this delicious fecundity, this fountain and spray of life, the fatal sterility of the male plunged itself, like a beak of brass, barren and bare. (37)

The passage is both critical of male interruption and highly sexualized in its language (Pratt; Vanita). "[P]our erect," "column of spray," and "spray of life" suggest male ejaculation yet describe Mrs. Ramsay. By contrast, the male actor in this passage, "the male [who] plunged," is characterized as sterile, violent, and unwelcome (see Stalla 29).

Woolf would explain this coupling of women's creativity and men's sterility more plainly in *A Room of One's Own*. Throughout history, she would argue, men's artistic success has owed a debt to the "highly developed creative faculty among women" (*A Room* 87) with whom men lived and on whom they depended for "some stimulus, some renewal of creative power" (86), which "would at once refresh and invigorate" them (86). In *To the Lighthouse* Mrs. Ramsay embodies this idea (Steinberg; N. Friedman; Blotner). She funnels her own creative powers into orchestrating successful dinner parties, caring for her children and the needy, and soothing her husband's bruised ego about his intellectual limitations. Yet the novel goes further with this idea, linking women who possess the creative faculty in an unnamed alliance.

Lily experiences her "moments of being" while attempting to paint Mrs. Ramsay for the first time. As she suppresses her "consciousness of outer things" (159), including the voices of others and her own sense of individual identity, she achieves the harmonious state necessary to create art, what twenty-first-century psychologists call "flow." "[H]er mind kept throwing up from its depths, scenes, and names, and sayings, and memories and ideas, like a fountain spurting over that glaring, hideously difficult white space, while she modelled it with greens and blues" (159). Here the empty white space of the canvas replaces the sterile male of the earlier passage. Both "beak of brass" (37) and "glaring, [. . .] white space" represent the forces, a husband's emotional demands and the female artist's anticipated or internalized male disapproval, that conspire to keep these women from satisfying their own creative desires. (For an alternative reading, see Doyle, "These Emotions" 56, 65; "Voyaging" 170–73.)

The final section of the novel, "The Lighthouse," brings an additional character into this fold: the Ramsays' youngest daughter, Cam, whom critics compare to Woolf (Spivak 39). Although not involved in creating art in any literal sense, while sailing to the lighthouse Cam experiences "moments of being" similar to those achieved by Lily and Mrs. Ramsay ten years prior. Suddenly, "[f]rom her hand, ice cold, held deep in the sea, there spurted up a fountain of joy at the change, at the escape, at the adventure (that she should be alive, that she should be there). And the drops falling from this sudden and unthinking fountain of joy fell here and there on the dark, the slumbrous shapes in her mind [. . .]" (189). As was true of her mother's and Lily's experiences, Cam feels a shower of intense delight saturate the disparate memories, thoughts, and sights forming in her mind.

Yet, even during her moment of exhilaration, Cam harbors some existential doubt. She wonders whether the isle on which their summer house rests, "had [. . .] a place in the universe—even that little island?" (189). Literally, Cam's vision of her home place has shrunken to the size of a tiny leaf from her perspective in the sailboat. Figuratively, "that little island" refers to not simply the Isle of Skye but by extension the British Isles more broadly. Here, although still uncertain, Cam appears to be regaining her sense of equilibrium after an even more disconcerting moment of crisis earlier in the voyage. Mr. Ramsay had fiercely chided her for not knowing the points of the compass. "He thought, women are always like that. [. . .] They could not keep anything clearly fixed in their minds" (167). Her father's condescension toward women generally coupled with his pathetic demonstration of self-pity and expectation that women should cater to him had, just a few minutes ago, "outraged her" (166). She recalls her upbringing in a family stifled by her father's patriarchal rule. "[T]hat crass blindness and tyranny of his [. . .] had poisoned her childhood and raised bitter storms, so that even now she woke in the night trembling with rage and remembered some command of his; some insolence: 'Do this,' 'Do that,' his dominance: his 'Submit to me'" (170).

The silent pact she has made with her younger brother, James, to "fight tyranny to the death" (168) begins to unravel, however, as her perspective broadens, and her thoughts turn to her father's gentleness and reassuring wisdom. "And watching her father as he wrote in his study, she thought (now sitting in the boat) he was not vain, nor a tyrant and did not wish to make you pity him. Indeed, if he saw she was there, reading a book, he would ask her, as gently as any one could, Was there nothing he could give her?" (189–90). The "fountain of joy" (189) she experiences sailing to the lighthouse engenders a more nuanced view of her father's character than was possible before (Goldman, *Feminist*).

As the sailors draw nearer to the lighthouse, James has the opportunity to experience a moment resembling Cam's. He steers the sailboat smoothly and, to his delight, wins his father's praise (206). Yet, having had to wait a lifetime for Mr. Ramsay's approval, James remains "sulky and frowning" to hide his pleasure (206). The opportunity of the moment fades. Instead of James's experiencing this moment of ecstasy, the physical environment registers its possibility. The boat demonstrates "an extraordinary lilt and exhilaration" denied expression by James (206). The sea creates an actual fountain, which parallels the figurative ones Mrs. Ramsay, Lily, and Cam experienced in their moments of reverie: "a wave incessantly broke

and spurted a little column of drops which fell down in a shower"
(206). James, whose mother predicted would become an artist, does
not join the creative coterie.

"Unclassified Affections"

That the characters included in this special circle are all female and
perceive the world differently from their male companions—
Mr. Ramsay, Mr. Bankes, and James, respectively—deserves attention. Woolf establishes an affiliation between Mrs. Ramsay and Lily,
and, belatedly, between them and Cam, based on their shared perspective of life's ephemeral beauty realized in their moments of
being. Interestingly, in the holograph draft of *To the Lighthouse*, the
working-class, presumably Irish (or Scottish) "Mrs. McNab *is*
'the fountain of life'" (Marcus, "Taking" 153; see, also, To the Lighthouse*: Original* TTL/Page 213 [MS 3.57]).

The notion that these multigenerational, middle-class Englishwomen share some indeterminate bond is established first and
foremost, however, through Lily Briscoe. In "The Window" section
(48–52), the novel offers glimpses into Lily's imagination as she struggles to understand Mrs. Ramsay and to reconcile the conflicting
emotions of love and frustration she engenders in Lily. Whereas
William Bankes admires Mrs. Ramsay for what he sees as her "perfect
shape" (49), that is, her conformity to established notions of feminine
beauty, including how they are manifested in fulfilling the roles of
wife and mother, Lily observes her subject through a "different ray"
(48). She wants to explore Mrs. Ramsay's difference from such perfection by observing her "relations with women" (49). Woolf describes
Lily's different way of seeing Mrs. Ramsay in an earlier draft of
the novel: "She was the very opposite of" how Mr. Bankes saw her,
"submissive, devoted, sublime"; at least with women, Mrs. Ramsay
was "wilful & commanding" (To the Lighthouse*: Original* TTL/Page
88 [MS 1.179]).

Lily's desire to see the imperfections, in effect to know the essence
of Mrs. Ramsay, sparks a fantasy in Lily about Mrs. Ramsay's visiting
her late at night (most critics discuss this scene as a memory; see, for
example, Doyle, "These Emotions" 55–56). Lily's imagined encounter
with Mrs. Ramsay begins with the parenthetical phrase "([s]o she
tried to start the tune of Mrs. Ramsay in her head)" (*To the Lighthouse* 49) and is further indicated by Woolf's use of the conditional

voice, as in such phrases as "she [Mrs. Ramsay] would adroitly shape" (49) and "Lily would say" (50). In Lily's extended fantasy, a kind of moving *tableau vivant* ("living picture"), Mrs. Ramsay, "wrapped in an old fur coat" (49), visits her in her room and reveals to Lily her private self. With Lily seated "on the floor with her arms round Mrs. Ramsay's knees" (50) and "her head on Mrs. Ramsay's lap" (50) "close as she could get" (51), Lily imagines that the two women talk until dawn, sharing an extended moment of intimacy.

First Lily considers and then rejects the idea that the intimacy she seeks with Mrs. Ramsay involves surreptitiously "press[ing] through into those secret chambers" of Mrs. Ramsay's "mind and heart" without her permission (51). That type of knowledge—which she compares to gaining access to sacred texts buried next to the bodies of dead kings (51)—resembles theft more than exchange. And any model of human intimacy in which connections are forged through the intellect alone fails to achieve a lasting union. As mentor and mentee, respectively, Mr. Ramsay and Charles Tansley share such relations; before he married, so too did Mr. Ramsay with William Bankes (21; see Vanita). However, "it was not knowledge but unity that she desired, not inscriptions on tablets, nothing that could be written in any language known to men, but intimacy itself [. . .]" (51; see Stalla 27, 31). The word "men" in place of the universal "man" indicates a gendered distinction as if to say that the connection Lily seeks with Mrs. Ramsay stands outside men's intelligibility (for a contrasting interpretation, see Oxindine 55). It defies codification within society's established signifying systems. It cannot be articulated let alone imagined by men.

Lily settles on a metaphor to describe her desire for intimacy with Mrs. Ramsay that is in keeping with the watery imagery and flowing rhythms of the novel. She longs to merge with Mrs. Ramsay mentally and physically, "becoming, like waters poured into one jar, inextricably the same, one with the object one adored [. . .]" (51). With its similar yet separate substances mingling together in a shared vessel, this image suggests mutuality as well as flow. It also reflects and anticipates Mrs. Ramsay's and Lily's separate yet parallel moments of ecstasy, "like a fountain spurting" (159), as discussed above. Though Lily will continue to the end of the novel "to want and want and not to have" (202) "the object one adored" (51), she realizes that "[l]ove had a thousand shapes. There might be lovers whose gift it was to choose out the elements of things and place them together and so, giving them a wholeness not theirs in life, make of some scene, or meeting of people (all now gone and separate), one of those globed compacted things over which thought lingers, and love plays" (192). Lily expresses her love for Mrs. Ramsay by completing her painting—itself a "gift" and "one of those globed compacted things" inspired by her particular vision of Mrs. Ramsay.

The artist Lily sees in Mrs. Ramsay what Woolf saw in Vita Sackville-West: beauty, maturity, willfulness, "splendour," "her capacity [. . .] to take the floor in any company," "maternal protection," "her being in short (what I have never been) a real woman" (*Diary* 3: 52; Raitt, *Vita* 158–67). For Lily and Woolf, extraordinary women provided the stimulus needed, the "sense of unity and coherency" necessary to create art (*Letters* 4: 200; DeSalvo, "Lighting" 197). (For a discussion of Woolf's anxieties about "maternal women," including her servant Nellie Boxall, see Light, 216–21.)

At the beginning of her love affair with Vita Sackville-West, minutes after Sackville-West left on a four-month trip to Persia (Iran), Woolf reflected on the temporary loss of this new "stimulus" in her life (*Diary* 3: 57; DeSalvo, "Lighting" 204; see, also, Stalla 27). The feeling of stimulation Sackville-West provided fused in Woolf's mind with "the invigoration" she felt about starting *To the Lighthouse* (*Diary* 3: 57). "All these fountains play on my being & intermingle" (*Diary* 3: 57). Near the end of their love affair, shortly after returning from a weeklong holiday together in Burgundy, France, unaccompanied by either of their husbands, Woolf wrote Vita Sackville-West a letter depicting what their relationship meant to her, using a familiar image: "How I watched you! How I felt—now what was it like! Well, somewhere I have seen a little ball kept bubbling up and down on the spray of a fountain: the fountain is you; the ball me. It is a sensation I get only from you. It is physically stimulating, restful at the same time [. . .]" (3: 540).

That Woolf envisioned her lover as "the spray of a fountain" that buoyed her, providing both stimulation and calm, adds a rich context for interpreting the ecstatic moments in *To the Lighthouse* experienced by Mrs. Ramsay, Lily, and Cam. (For a related discussion of Nancy Ramsay's epiphany, see Oxindine 56–58.) To classify these moments, or for that matter Woolf's affections for Sackville-West, as merely sexual limits their significance—although the sexualized language used to describe them is palpable. Likewise to ignore the period of erotic rapture in which Woolf composed *To the Lighthouse* or Lily's love for Mrs. Ramsay represented therein would limit our understanding of the novel. The fountain spray these female characters experience during their private ecstasies evokes the excitement Woolf felt in the company of women she adored. It was a sensation matched only by the exhilaration she got from writing. Indeed, as noted above, the two sensations flowed together (Raitt, *Vita* 161). Beloved women and writing satisfied Woolf in a way that nothing else in her life did.

Political Silences

Readers disconcerted by the interpretation outlined above may be similarly dismayed by political critiques of *To the Lighthouse* that engage the issues of war and empire. These interpretive schemas are less apparent than readings focused on heterosexual marriage and the female artist. In fact, they require approaching the novel as a palimpsest with several layers of meaning. Peal away the top layers, that is, the textual meanings most immediately recognizable, and the novel reveals several submerged stories.

Early critics of Woolf, who characterized her literary concerns as being purely aesthetic, created the impetus for these relatively recent interpretations that recognize Woolf's political preoccupations, such as women's rights, pacifism, and anti-fascism. Initial feminist analyses of *To the Lighthouse*, for example, precipitated myriad critiques of gender politics in the novel in relation to the institutions of the bourgeois family, war, race, and empire (see, for example, Doyle, "These Emotions," "Voyaging"; Emery; Phillips; S. Friedman; Seshagiri). In chapter 4, I will summarize these arguments. Here, I wish to examine select passages that lend themselves to this type of political reading.

The "Time Passes" section of *To the Lighthouse* offers the most direct route into the political schema focused on war and empire. As discussed in chapter 2, "Time Passes" exemplifies the extremity of Woolf's experimental prose style in *To the Lighthouse*, a style that would reach its peak in Woolf's novel *The Waves* (1931). The central characters of this section are Mrs. McNab, the house, and the elements of nature—the former two serving as co-protagonists and the latter, as antagonist. As explained above, truths as seemingly unshakeable as the beauty of nature and the nature of beauty are suddenly disturbed by the violence of the Great War (Levenback). "Time Passes" represents the decade leading up to and including World War I as a period in which "no light of reason" (134) ruled the universe (see Spivak 35–38). In a scenario of nature out of control, plants grow wild, battling human habitation and unnaturally reproducing to the point that "the poppy seed[ed] itself and the carnation mate[d] with the cabbage" (138). Once serene vistas of the sea blush purple, stained with soldiers' blood (133–34). Even seemingly unalterable forces, such as "the winds and waves," mimic the "idiot games," "brute confusion and wanton lust" played out on the battlefield (134–35).

This submerged story about the War, with its oblique yet implicit pacifist message, links up with and expands the meaning of other passages in the novel that critique the violence of everyday life. For example, James determines to "track down and stamp out—tyranny, [and] despotism" by resisting the imperious demands of his father (184). Lily Briscoe defies expected gender roles by refusing—first with Charles Tansley at the dinner table and later with Mr. Ramsay and his boots—to place men's needs above her own (Weil; for an alternate reading, see Doyle, "Voyaging" 169–70). James's conviction that "[i]t was in this world that the wheel went over the person's foot" turning it "purple, crushed" (185) and the "fierce sudden black-winged harpy [. . .] struck and struck [. . .]" (184) suggests a brutal underside to domestic life. By linking the repressive gender roles propagated by the family in the name of love to the "idiot games" perpetrated by the military in the name of patriotism, *To the Lighthouse* extends its political critique beyond women's and children's oppression and middle-class domestic life.

Postcolonial readings of *To the Lighthouse* build on this connection further by examining, for example, how the rhetoric of empire used in the novel points to a submerged story of global domination that parallels the book's domestic narrative (see McVicker, "Reading"; Doyle, "Voyaging"; Phillips; Winston; Seshagiri; Stalla). After all, the notion of the middle-class English family as a harmonious hub provided an appealing metaphor for late-nineteenth- and early-twentieth-century British imperialist propaganda that posited England and her Queen as the mother, and the colonies and colonized as (often unruly) children. Allusions to foreign gains, imperial relations, and racial metaphors punctuate *To the Lighthouse*. Lily's Chinese eyes assume new meaning by marking the woman artist as foreigner within this motherland. The "bones [that] bleach and burn far away in Indian sands" (127) in "Time Passes" refer specifically to

Britain's destruction of India's cotton industry, which created widespread famine throughout this supposed "jewel" in the Empire's "crown" (Winston). The "opal necklace, which Uncle James had brought her [Mrs. Ramsay] from India" (80–81), and the "beast's skull" that hangs in the nursery, "[s]hot in foreign parts no doubt," hint at imperial conquest and plunder (140; Phillips; Winston).

If *To the Lighthouse* assigns blame anywhere for such violence, then it is with Mr. Ramsay and men of his generation and social class, whose "admirable fabric of the masculine intelligence" was responsible for "upholding the world"—literally running England and her colonies (106; McVicker, "Vast"; "Reading"). Even seemingly polite gestures, such as Mr. Ramsay's chivalry toward women, which his wife admires, are implicated in this global system of domination (98–99).

Be that as it may, the novel suggests that Englishwomen, too, not merely participate in but actively uphold Britain's imperialist system (Doyle, "Voyaging"; Phillips; Winston). Mrs. Ramsay lets men's political vision of the world "uphold her and sustain her" (106) even as she sustains men through her beauty, sympathy, and deference to masculine authority. "Indeed, she had the whole of the other sex under her protection; for reasons she could not explain, for their chivalry and valour, for the fact that they negotiated treaties, ruled India, controlled finance [. . .]" (6). In a sense, Mrs. Ramsay supports the men and the system ruling India by assuming her role as sympathetic wife and mother. She then encourages her husband, family, and friends to reproduce the existing social order by insisting "they all must marry" (49).

More than a decade after publishing *To the Lighthouse*, and on the brink of another world war, Woolf presented her political views on the global crises of war, imperialism, and fascism in a book-length essay, *Three Guineas* (1938), in which she calls for women to form a "Society of Outsiders" (199) in defiance of Britain's patriarchal rule. As evidenced from her having written this polemical work and her comments in letters of this period, Woolf in later life appears to have concluded that the artist's responsibility to society in times of impending war was to continue to create art. In fact Woolf hints that she believed art might save society from the ills of militarism and authoritarianism if only politicians fulfilled their duties to its citizenry by mandating adequate universal education that included literature and art appreciation (*Letters* 6: 414–15, 419–21, 421–22).

The idea that art and thought are not only necessary for human survival but also actually instrumental in creating a peaceful and just society finds its way into *To the Lighthouse*. When Lily Briscoe hears Charles Tansley lecturing on "brotherly love" during the War, she cannot help wondering, "how could he love his kind who did not know one picture from another" (197) and who mocked women for being artists? And when she considers Mrs. Ramsay's ministrations to the sick and poor, Lily reflects on "the ineffectiveness of action, the supremacy of thought" (196). The pacifist politics embedded in *To the Lighthouse*, then, critique patriarchal rule and military violence as mutually supporting forces of chaos and repression. Only the New Woman, the artist, offers an alternative "vision" (209).

TOPICS FOR FURTHER DISCUSSION

The Lighthouse

When asked by her friend Roger Fry what the lighthouse symbolized in *To the Lighthouse*, Woolf replied, "I meant *nothing* by The Lighthouse. One has to have a central line down the middle of the book to hold the design together. I saw that all sorts of feelings would accrue to this, but I refused to think them out, and trusted that people would make it the deposit for their own emotions—[. . .]" (*Letters* 3: 385). As explained in Chapter 1, Woolf based the lighthouse in the novel on childhood memories of her beloved Godrevy Lighthouse off the coast of St. Ives. As an adult revisiting the area of her youth, she refers to it passionately in journals and letters as "my Lighthouse" (*Letters* 4: 165; 5: 213), a gleaming figure (*Passionate* 299) "seen as through steamy glass" (*Letters* 1: 416). We know, too, that she compared her lover, Vita Sackville-West, to a lighthouse, for her self-possession, remoteness, and beauty.

The lighthouse figures prominently throughout the novel. It is included in every section, and we are reminded of its presence repeatedly as individual characters reflect on its changing appearance. The phallic shape of the lighthouse has led some critics to associate it with masculine authority (Empson). Such a reading is consistent with interpretations of the novel that emphasize the "marriage of opposites" theme. The waves, which surround the lighthouse, are then read as a symbol of femininity and together suggest a harmonious androgyny.

Additionally, as the end point in this quest narrative, the light-house is linked to Mr. Ramsay's goal-oriented approach to life, including his pursuit of philosophical truth and professional success. Speaking generally of the quest narrative, the male character fulfills his quest and thereby achieves manhood. *To the Lighthouse* under-cuts this aim, however, by James's particular triumph as he approaches and eventually reaches his longed for destination. "So that was the Lighthouse, was it? No, the other was also the Lighthouse. For noth-ing was simply one thing" (186). The actual lighthouse is rather ordinary, James finds, a barred structure showing signs of human habitation, unlike the fantasy lighthouse of his childhood imagina-tion. Yet, he concludes that both visions are accurate, showing him to be more of the artist than the goal-oriented academic. The starkness of the tower, which "confirmed some obscure feeling of his about his own character" (203), and his realization, as he recites a line from one of his father's favorite poems, William Cowper's "The Castaway," that "'We are driving before a gale—we must sink'" (203) suggest James's recognition that we live and die alone. Instead of slaying one's enemies, the goal of this quest narrative, then, is to realize life's multiplicity, including that one's father is not simply a brute (Roberts, "Toward"; N. Friedman; Henke).

Despite this association between the lighthouse and male identity formation, Kathleen McKenna points to the autoerotically charged connection between the lighthouse and Mrs. Ramsay (30–32; see, also, Pratt; Spivak; Jacobus). In an early scene, Mrs. Ramsay feels caught, as if she were at the mercy of the lighthouse's steady demanding beam, which shines into her window from across the sea. Slowly, the rhythmic stroking of the light begins to hypnotize and soothe her to the point of private ecstasy (65). The language used to describe Mrs. Ramsay's encounter with the lighthouse beam—"bursting," "flood," "waves of pure delight" (65)—resembles the earlier scene of Mrs. Ramsay's rap-ture discussed in detail above. Laura Doyle, for whom Mrs. Ramsay's relationship to the lighthouse beam is described as one between a woman and her demanding male lover, nonetheless reads this scene as "affirm[ing] Mrs. Ramsay's sexual pleasure in that [heterosexual] relationship—a pleasure distinctively clitoral, distinctively feminine" ("These Emotions" 53; see, also, "Voyaging" 153–55).

In this scene the lighthouse illumines two seemingly incompatible states of consciousness emphasized throughout the novel. The light beats the steady rhythm of time, thus marking the limits of human mortality, and it appears to stop time by stimulating in the observer a heightened state of awareness whereby quotidian concerns vanish and life's magnificence shines forth. Noting the lighthouse beams' function to "measure time in terms of light," biographer Julia Briggs associates the lighthouse "with isolation and, by extension, the inner life, as well as with the saving power of light that opposes the flood of darkness in 'Time Passes'" (*Virginia Woolf* 181–82). "[I]ts three beams correspond to the structure of the novel—two long beams, one of them Mrs. Ramsay's, and a short beam" (Briggs, *Virginia Woolf* 182).

If one were to follow Woolf's lead and make the lighthouse "the deposit for their [readers'] own emotions," then what do you believe the lighthouse signifies in *To the Lighthouse*? To get started, identify all of the passages in the novel in which the lighthouse is mentioned. Reread these passages closely, and determine what the lighthouse means within each of these individual passages. Next, consider all of your close readings together, and try to formulate a meaning of the lighthouse that makes sense in every case.

DISCUSSION QUESTIONS

1. Woolf commented in her diary that she wanted the sound of the sea to be heard throughout *To the Lighthouse* (3: 34). Did she achieve this goal? If so, where in the novel do you hear the sea? What literary devices does Woolf employ to create this effect? What meaning does this aural embellishment contribute to the novel in relation to its other meanings? You may want to compare the places in the novel where you can hear the sea to those passages in which characters comment about seeing the sea.

2. Numerous passages in the novel portray characters reflecting on their changing visual perspectives from one moment to the next. For example, Cam looks at a tide pool (75–76) and her house from the sailboat (165–66); Mrs. Ramsay looks at the dinner party guests around the table through candlelight (97); Lily Briscoe looks at the sailboat carrying the Ramsays to the lighthouse (188, 191–92); James looks at the lighthouse (203–04); and Mr. Ramsay looks at the island (207). At other points in the novel, characters' perspectives overlap so that it becomes difficult to determine where one character's thoughts leave off and another's begin (see Auerbach). This is particularly true for scenes involving Mrs. Ramsay and Lily. Carefully reread several of these specific passages. What do they contribute to

the theme of multiple perspectives explored in the novel? How are the novel's experiments with narrative point of view similar and different from Lily's distinctive way of seeing and painting as a modernist artist?

3. Analyze the "Time Passes" section. Why do you think Woolf chose to bracket off important events, such as the deaths of Mrs. Ramsay, Andrew, and Prue? What effect does such bracketing have on you as you read this section? How are the characters Mrs. McNab, Mrs. Bast, and George Bast represented? How do their characterizations contrast with those of the Ramsays and their guests in "The Window" section? Other than that they are brought in to ready the Ramsay house, what *literary* functions do Mrs. McNab, Mrs. Bast, and George Bast serve? (For answers to these questions, see Emery; for biographical and historical contexts, see Flint; MacKay; Light.)

4. We know that Woolf wrote *To the Lighthouse* to put to rest the memory of her parents, Leslie and Julia Stephen. Death is a recurrent theme in the novel. Sailing to the lighthouse, Mr. Ramsay takes "pleasure in memory of dead people" (165) as Macalister, the local boatman, recounts the "[t]hree [ships that] had sunk" nearby (164). In "Time Passes," Mrs. McNab does not merely recall Mrs. Ramsay before her employer's death but also can actually "see her [. . .] stooping over her flowers [. . .] with one of the children by her [. . .]" (136). And at the end of the novel, Lily sees a vision of Mrs. Ramsay "raising to her forehead a wreath of white flowers," "stepping [. . .] across fields" "with her companion" (181). Discuss the novel as a *memento mori*, a reminder of death (literally translated from the Latin as "remember that you must die"). Examine closely these particular scenes, and identify others that comment on death and mortality.

CHAPTER 4

CRITICAL RECEPTION AND PUBLISHING HISTORY

Virginia Woolf . . . has now become the reigning goddess of contemporary English letters. Her novels sell even when the buyer knows, either from past experience or from reviews, that he probably will not understand them. Now specialists begin to write interpretations, offering to the "common reader" guides and suggestions toward comprehension. She is talked about everywhere: . . . almost universally with adoration.
  —John Hawley Roberts, "Toward Virginia Woolf," 1934, Virginia
Quarterly Review

I am sure that certain critics will instantly object that Mrs. Woolf is extremely insignificant—that she is a purely feminist phenomenon— that she is taken seriously by no one any longer today . . . and that, anyway, feminism is a dead issue. . . . [W]hile I am ready to agree that the intrinsic importance of Mrs. Woolf may be exaggerated by her friends, I cannot agree that as a symbolic landmark—a sort of party-lighthouse—she has not a very real significance. And she has crystallized for us . . . what is in fact the feminine—as distinguished from the feminist—standpoint.
  —Wyndham Lewis, 1934, Men Without Art

Writing in 1934, midpoint between *To the Lighthouse*'s publication and Woolf's death in 1941, U.S. scholar John Hawley Roberts and English Vorticist artist Wyndham Lewis offer antithetical assessments of Woolf's critical merit and acclaim. Their comments exemplify important aspects of the history of criticism of Virginia Woolf's writings, or at least as that history is born out in responses to *To the*

Lighthouse. First, this critical history is fraught with heated disagreement. Secondly, Woolf's position as both a woman writer and a feminist features prominently in reviews of her work from the beginning. Finally, Woolf's celebrity status incites indignation in some, curiosity in others. Certain themes, debates, and controversies predominate in Woolf criticism. Is she a minor or a major writer? Does her prose reflect a specifically feminine style? Is her fiction solely concerned with aesthetics, or is it in fact daringly political? Are her characters and plots "bloodless" (Swinnerton, Review 442) and sexless, or are sexuality and gender central to her literary concerns?

The reader new to Woolf, or at least to her novel *To the Lighthouse*, should take comfort in several facts about the critical responses. Hundreds of essays have been written about the novel, many offering widely divergent interpretations. In their explanations of its central themes and their explications of specific scenes, these critiques taken together suggest the multiplicity of meanings possible. The consequence of such diversity of interpretation is that any attempt to discover *the* correct meaning is not only impossible but also meaningless. The reader instead creates meaning for him- or herself, using the tools of literary interpretation: close reading, precise analysis, and rigorous research to contextualize the novel.

Although critics have been writing about *To the Lighthouse* for nearly a century, particular themes resonate throughout its long history. Because of the sheer volume of critical responses after Woolf's death, I have organized my discussion around specific aspects of the novel, clustering ideas into central motifs and symbols as well as reigning interpretations and critical disputes. I will begin, however, with an overview of how *To the Lighthouse* was received during Woolf's lifetime, beginning upon first publication.

EVERYTHING SEEMS WITHIN REACH

Within weeks after its publication in England by the Hogarth Press on 5 May 1927, *To the Lighthouse* became a commercial and critical success (see Briggs, *Virginia Woolf* 186). In a letter to her friend and former Greek tutor, Janet Case, Woolf writes, "Everything seems to be within ones [sic] reach [. . .]" (3: 403). Woolf was pleased with her new novel, especially the dinner party scene, and she delighted in its pre- and post-publication sales, which made it her most popular book to date (see *Diary* 3: 134, 136, 147; *Letters* 3: 403). The large sales and mostly laudatory press reviews helped bolster Woolf's confidence that she had succeeded in her radical literary experiment. Just one month after its release, *To the Lighthouse* had received so much positive public attention that Woolf felt emboldened to write in her diary, "I think, however, I am now almost an established figure—as a writer. They dont [sic] laugh at me any longer. [. . .] Possibly I shall be a celebrated writer. Anyhow, The Lighthouse is much more nearly a success, in the usual sense of the word, than any other book of mine" (3: 137).

Woolf's friends unanimously praised her achievement. The poet Stephen Spender thought it "delightful" (qtd. in V. Woolf, *Letters* 5: 314 n1); E. M. Forster remarked on its beauty, adding that "it stirs me much more to questions of whether & why than anything else you have written" (qtd. in V. Woolf, *Diary* 3: 137 n3); Vita Sackville-West felt "dazzled and bewitched" by it (196); the art critic Roger Fry proclaimed the novel to be "the best thing you've done" (qtd. in Q. Bell, *Virginia Woolf* 2: 128); Leonard Woolf declared it to be a "psychological poem" and a "masterpiece" (qtd. in V. Woolf, *Diary* 3: 123); most importantly to Woolf, Vanessa Bell commended her sister for "hav[ing] given a portrait of mother which is more like her to me than anything I could ever have conceived possible" (V. Bell, *Selected Letters* 317).

Even before the novel's debut in England, however, Woolf garnered attention for her experimental prose by publishing an earlier version of "Time Passes" in the Parisian journal *Commerce*, the first of her writings to be published in French (Briggs, *Virginia Woolf* 183). Roger Fry and E. M. Forster's friend Charles Mauron, who had translated Forster's *A Passage to India* into French and who would later translate *Orlando* and *Flush* as well as write psychological criticism on the French symbolist poet Stéphane Mallarmé, translated Woolf's typescript of "Time Passes" ["Le temps passe"] in time for the journal's winter issue published in December 1926 (Haule, "'Le Temps passe'" 267, 275 n4; Briggs, *Virginia Woolf* 447 n116; Hutcheon 207–08). Comparing the English typescript Woolf sent to Mauron to both the holograph draft of *To the Lighthouse* and its U.K. and U.S. published versions, critic James Haule concludes that this "intermediary" version (270) of "Time Passes"—which is more abstract overall and which omits the characters from "The Window," including the parenthetical mention of Mrs. Ramsay's, Prue Ramsay's, and Andrew Ramsay's deaths (271)—represents "human disintegration and despair and . . . the significance of insignificant labor" more unrelentingly than does the middle section of Woolf's published novel ("'Le Temps passe'" 269, 274). *To the Lighthouse* was well received in France because "from the outset, certain French critics seemed to recognize exactly what she was doing" (Briggs, *Virginia Woolf* 183–84). The French appreciation for this "definitive work," which is "so full and so luminous," culminated in 1928 (Mayoux 214). *To the Lighthouse* received the Femina Vie Heureuse prize—awarded annually to "a strong and original piece of work, excellent in matter and in style, promising for the future, and calculated to reveal to French readers the true spirit and character of England" ("Femina").

Most early book reviewers and literary critics, writing between May 1927 and March 1941, recognize *To the Lighthouse* to be Woolf's best novel. Nearly everyone commends the artistry of Woolf's technique displayed in *To the Lighthouse*. For example, the anonymous book reviewer for the *Times Literary Supplement* (London) mentions the novel's "piquancy and poetry" and "the charm and pleasure of her [Woolf's] design" ("Mrs. Woolf's New Novel" 315). Conrad Aiken, writing in the literary journal *The Dial*, remarks that in *To the Lighthouse* Woolf has perfected her method to the point that the reader aptly loses consciousness of it: "The technical brilliance glows, melts, falls away; and there remains a poetic apprehension of life of extraordinary loveliness" (17). A counterpoint to Aiken, William Empson praises Woolf's "poetical use of language" in *To the Lighthouse* but warns that her method rings false in particular passages in "Time Passes" where the moods expressed reflect the author's feelings instead of those of her characters (208). As to Woolf's experimental method in *To the Lighthouse*, critics use various terms to describe it: "modern" (Muller 32), "impressionist" (Muller 32; Empson 214; Swinnerton, *Georgian* 376), "subjective or 'confessional'" (Troy 87); her focus on characters' internal thoughts is described variously as "stream" or "flux of consciousness" (Muller 30; Aiken 17), "associative train of thought" (Roberts, "Toward" 591), "interior monologue" (Muller 30), or, simply, "self-consciousness" (Aiken 16).

WOMAN WRITER

These early commentators recurrently discuss Woolf's writing in relation to the subjects of sex, gender, and feminism, demonstrating the origins, and long history, of such themes within studies of Woolf's work. Several critics characterize Woolf's fictional prose style as "feminine" (Aiken 16; Muller 35) or use expressions associated with femininity, often with pejorative implications, to describe her style, subject matter, characters, or even the author herself. Words and phrases such as "delicacy" (Empson 212, 215; Muller 31), "submissive sensitiveness" (Empson 212), "sentimental evasion" (Beach 611), "flutterings of . . . fancy" (Swinnerton, *Georgian* 374), "preciosity," "fussiness," and "fragil[ity]" (Muller 32, 35) pepper these early responses. Herbert Muller sums up this pervasive sentiment, which he finds applicable both to Woolf and to modern women writers generally: "the mere man still yearns for a little red beef"; in other words, women's writing is, lamentably, not sufficiently "masculine" (Muller 35).

Along these same lines, several critics charge that Woolf's writing lacks vitality on the grounds that life's physical, as opposed to mental, realities remain unexplored (Muller 32; Swinnerton, *Georgian* 374–75). The lack of dramatic action derived from a strong plot dissatisfies them. The genteel domestic settings and her characters' rarified lives, ostensibly sheltered from real-world calamities, rankle (Beach 611; Muller 33; Troy 87–88). Also disliked is Woolf's preference for portraying hypersensitive intellectuals and eschewing strong gender distinctions (Beach 610–12).

Departing from the sexism rife within these early responses to Woolf's work, John Hawley Roberts instead praises Woolf's "conception of character in fiction" as "her chief attribute"; he recognizes that her "abstraction of character . . . [is] a means toward greater intensity" not less ("Toward" 587, 589). Writing in 1934, he also appears to be the first literary critic to appreciate Woolf's approach to issues of sex, sexuality, and gender. As if responding directly to the criticisms of his contemporaries, Roberts explains: "But, one may ask, what about sex? Does it not belong in the design? Mrs. Woolf must answer, of course, that it does. . . . She sees it . . . as a contributory factor in her larger, more generalized problem" ("Toward" 594). He goes on to identify "bisexual[ity]" (595) in Woolf's novel *Mrs. Dalloway* (1925) as a preamble to explaining the transgendered reality of human nature that Woolf represents in her characters:

> "Male and female created He them," is a pronouncement Mrs. Woolf does not believe in. The sexual characteristics are not so easily catalogued; male and female, like hate and love, are only

two phases of the same thing and not clearly distinguishable. . . .
[A] novelist dealing with life itself, as distinct from an externalized
character, must show how masculine and feminine . . . merge
and intermingle. This interest in double sex is a recurrent one in
Mrs. Woolf's work. ("Toward" 595)

FROM "DOUBLE SEX" TO "DOUBLE VISION" AND "ANDROGYNY": POST-1941 ANALYSES

After Woolf's death on 28 March 1941, her literary status fluctuated
although "with F. R. Leavis ruling the British critical scene . . . and
the New Critics ruling the American one, Woolf was generally deni-
grated as an aesthete and her work labeled minor" (Daugherty and
Pringle 9). However, Erich Auerbach's essay "The Brown Stocking,"
the final chapter of his seminal book *Mimesis: The Representation of
Reality in Western Literature* (first published in German in 1946 and
translated into English in 1953), would help secure *To the Lighthouse*'s
place in the literary canon (Caughie, "Returning" 49–50). Auerbach's
formalist reading focuses on Woolf's innovative coupling of multiple
characters' shifting consciousnesses and "the contrast between 'exterior' and 'interior' time" (475) with an iconoclastic "attitude toward
the reality of the world" represented in the novel (472). As Auerbach
describes, "the exterior events have actually lost their hegemony, they
serve to release and interpret inner events . . ." (475).

Auerbach's characterization of *To the Lighthouse* as representative
of "the realistic novel of the era between the two great wars" (482)
for its structural concerns contrasts with John Hawley Roberts's
focus on Woolf's representation of bisexuality and her belief in the
"double sex," that is, not just the presence but also the desirability of
both masculine and feminine qualities within the same individual.
Roberts's emphasis on *To the Lighthouse* and gender prefigured
numerous critical interpretations that would follow. For many critics,
Mr. and Mrs. Ramsay represent the two necessary components of
either a successful marriage or a complete human being: intellec-
tualism/logic and creativity/intuition. Depending on which critic
you believe, these qualities fuse together harmoniously in Mr. and
Mrs. Ramsay's marriage, in Lily Briscoe, or in Mrs. Ramsay.

For example, Mr. and Mrs. Ramsay represent the complementarity
of the sexes in Joan Bennett's book *Virginia Woolf: Her Art as a
Novelist* (1945). "When there is love between a man and a woman . . .

the differences between them become contributory to a whole. . . . So it is with . . . Mr and Mrs Ramsay [sic]" (83). However, "[t]hese different kinds of consciousness supplement as well as oppose each other," according to Howard Brogan in "Science and Narrative Structure in Austen, Hardy, and Woolf" (1957) (283). For Brogan, rather than the Ramsays' union, it is "Lily [who] unites these disparate elements by a single line [in her painting] which apparently represents herself as the artist detached from the process of living, moved to her work by the aesthetic significance of Mrs. Ramsay, but understanding as Mrs. Ramsay had been unable to do the science and logic of the masculine mind" (284).

The differing conclusions critics reach about which character embodies the ideal mixture of animus and anima and where that is demonstrated in the novel become a debate over women's proper place in society. For those critics claiming Lily represents that ideal, the implication is that women should be allowed to develop their intellect and ambition as well as their emotions (Henke 43–44). For those critics favoring traditional gender roles, such as Herbert Marder in *Feminism and Art: A Study of Virginia Woolf* (1968), Mrs. Ramsay, in her womanly perfection as "wife, mother, hostess, . . . creating with the whole of her being," represents "the androgynous artist in life" by embodying a "wholeness" the other characters lack (128).

Yet not every interpretation of Mrs. Ramsay as androgynous emphasizes her "earth mother" adherence to conventional notions of femaleness (Heilbrun, *Toward* 156). In "Sexual Imagery in *To the Lighthouse*: A New Feminist Approach" (1972), Annis Pratt locates Mrs. Ramsay's androgyny, not in her functions as "wife, mother, hostess" as Marder does but instead, in her phallic female sexuality: "the column [of spray] in its erection and life-giving powers suggests a quest into the innermost reaches of Mrs. Ramsay's psyche, a consummation through her taking on both male and female sexual characteristics . . ." (425).

Other critics move beyond the intellectual/intuitive binary by seeing the novel's dualisms more abstractly. For example, according to Norman Friedman in "The Waters of Annihilation: Double Vision in *To the Lighthouse*"(1955), Mr. and Mrs. Ramsay are two characters out of many in the novel who must undergo a transformation so as to achieve a necessary synthesis of perspective, what Friedman calls the "double vision" (63). These characters make a "transition from the single view, whether it be that of objective detachment or subjective involvement, to the double vision which apprehends the nature of reality simultaneously from both points of view" (76).

Still others, influenced by feminist and poststructuralist theories, turn not to synthesis and a desire for wholeness but instead to thwarting the dualisms central to Western philosophy and supportive of patriarchy's "silencing objectification of women" (Doyle, "These Emotions" 42). For example, in "'These Emotions of the Body': Intercorporeal Narrative in *To The Lighthouse*" (1994), Laura Doyle, using the phenomenological theories of French philosopher Maurice Merleau-Ponty, argues that moments of bodily sensation registered when characters connect with inanimate objects, and through them, other characters, as well as the narrator's position not within but "*between* characters" (56) destabilize Western philosophy's privileging of spiritual and intellectual transcendence over corporeal, material realities (42–43, 56–57, 64–65). "Woolf's prose moves into the fleshy 'in-between' of her characters' fictional world, discovers its folds and ruptures, embraces its curves and arabesques. In short, far from maintaining the prudery or ethereality with which Woolf has often been identified, her narrative sensualizes metaphysical questions—of death and presence, speech and silence, time and space" (43).

THE OEDIPAL TRIANGLE

Although dualism and its accompanying struggles over synthesis, transcendence, and deconstruction figure prominently within discussions of *To the Lighthouse*, so too does triangulation. Numerous critics highlight what they see as the Oedipal relationship in *To the Lighthouse* among Mr. Ramsay, Mrs. Ramsay, and their youngest son, James. Reading the novel psychoanalytically, these critics conclude that James's hatred for his father and his fantasies of killing him are connected to, in the classic Freudian fashion, his strong attachment to his mother, for whose love and affection he and his father compete. What these critics determine to be the underlying causes of this triangulation and what they make of its significance to the novel's larger meanings, however, differ widely and depend upon how they respond to Mr. Ramsay and Mrs. Ramsay as individual characters.

For example, in "Vision in *To the Lighthouse*" (1958), Glenn Pedersen reads the novel as a story of a dysfunctional family dominated by a selfish, domineering matriarch, who refuses to relinquish her individuality and submit to her husband's desire for a conjugal relationship that elevates his needs above all others'. She accomplishes this by cultivating an unhealthy attachment to her youngest son. Only upon Mrs. Ramsay's death are James and his father able to form a normal bond, and is the family able to flourish, symbolized by their successful trip to the lighthouse (591).

Pedersen's reading is more the exception than the rule, however. From the first published responses to *To the Lighthouse* in 1927, most critics have considered Mr. Ramsay to be the impediment to family harmony as his own narcissism and rigidity of outlook prevent him from bonding with his children and enjoying life's interpersonal and sensory delights (Brogan 282). The 1927 anonymous book reviewer for the *Times Literary Supplement* refers to Mr. Ramsay as an "egotist," noting that "all the family have a sense of paternal tyranny" ("Mrs. Woolf's New Novel" 315). Nearly thirty years later, in his 1955 study of Leslie Stephen's influence on the development of Mr. Ramsay, Frank Baldanza describes Woolf's fictional character as "a rapacious tyrant" (550). Other critics use subtler language to describe Mr. Ramsay's part in the family drama. For Joseph Warren Beach, who considers Mr. Ramsay to be Woolf's most convincing fictional character, "the most interesting situation [in *To the Light-house*] is that involving him [Mr. Ramsay] and his son and daughter while on their sailing trip" "and how the intensity of the relation between him and his son grows out of their sharply defined rivalry for a woman's affection" (610 n3; see also Daiches 80–81; Roberts, "Vision" 846).

Emphasizing Mrs. Ramsay's role in the marriage, and her significance within the novel, as a creative, rather than a castrating, force, Erwin Steinberg, in "Freudian Symbolism and Communication" (1953), praises Woolf's effective use of phallic and fertility symbolism in *To the Lighthouse*. He interprets the passage in which Mrs. Ramsay's "fountain and spray of life" is penetrated by a "beak of brass" as symbolizing the heterosexual union and through it "Mr. Ramsay drawing new life from his wife" (V. Woolf, *To the Lighthouse* 37; Steinberg 5). Joseph Blotner, in "Mythic Patterns in *To the Lighthouse*" (1956), takes the idea of Mrs. Ramsay's fertility as central to the novel to its mythological conclusion. He asserts that *To the Lighthouse* draws from Greek mythology, with Mrs. Ramsay as Demeter to Lily Briscoe's Persephone (547, 556, 559 and 559 n14). Mrs. Ramsay signifies "[t]he feminine principle, the Kore" (559): "Her influence works toward the mating of men and women, toward their becoming fruitful like herself. Her function is the same on the intellectual level, for she gives her protection and inspiration to both art and science" (Blotner 550). According to Blotner, Mrs. Ramsay functions in the novel to enable her family to reach the lighthouse and Lily to finish her painting (559; see also Roberts, "Toward" 597; H. Russell Q2). More generally, as the embodiment of female power, Mrs. Ramsay counteracts "the effects of male violence, hate, and destructiveness" in the world (Blotner 562).

Mrs. Ramsay's type of female power comes with a heavy price, however, as feminist critics have been asserting at least since the 1970s: premature death, for one thing; little time to pursue her own passions, such as philanthropy, for another. Feminist critics open up a range of interpretations by focusing less attention on the hetero-sexual couple in *To the Lighthouse* and more on Mrs. Ramsay's relationship to Lily Briscoe and to her daughter Cam.

MOTHER-DAUGHTER RELATIONSHIPS

Both Mrs. Ramsay's relations with Cam and her bond with Lily Briscoe constitute mother-daughter relationships, according to several feminist critics (see, in particular, Marcus, "Taking"; Heilbrun, "*To the Lighthouse*"; Abel, *Virginia Woolf*; Froula). The biographical lens offers evidence to link Mrs. Ramsay's youngest daughter to Virginia Woolf, whose own ambivalence toward her parents is apparent in her journals, letters, and memoir and emerges fully when juxtaposed with Leslie Stephen's *Mausoleum Book*. As was true of Woolf, Cam comes to identify more with her father, the intellectual, than her mother, the beautiful Victorian "Angel in the House" although she deeply resents her father's histrionics and tyrannical demands for female sympathy. Some critics, Louise DeSalvo most notably in *Virginia Woolf: The Impact of Childhood Sexual Abuse on Her Life and Work*, read Cam's erratic behavior in *To the Lighthouse* in opposition to her mother's wishes, her fear of the boar's skull in the bedroom, and Mrs. Ramsay's distrust of her daughter's version of events as fictional manifestations of the real-life sexual abuse Woolf suffered as a child at the hands of her stepbrothers, Gerald and George Duckworth. The mother does not protect the girl-child from violation, and so she turns away from her but never develops her own strong sense of self (see, also, P. Bennett).

Lily Briscoe, as the artist figure and, arguably, the novel's protagonist, suggests to many critics, however, that she most closely represents the author. Jane Lilienfeld, in "'The Deceptiveness of Beauty':
Mother Love and Mother Hate in *To the Lighthouse*" (1977), offers
a compelling assessment of this correspondence when she argues
that "Lily Briscoe is herself a surrogate for the daughter, angry at
her mother's commitment to others, a daughter who sustains her
mother's death, and who lives beyond it to grow into her own person-
hood" (346). This growth is possible, Lilienfeld explains, only by
Lily's (and, by extension, Woolf's) developing "her mature assessment of Mrs. Ramsay" and, respectively, Julia Stephen, which
accounts for her imperfections as well as her magnificence (347).

LESBIAN AND GAY READINGS

Lilienfeld, along with other feminist critics, rescues Lily from a life
within Woolf criticism of either failed femininity or perpetual
virginity. Many scholars, particularly those publishing in the 1940s
and '50s, have refused to recognize Lily's unmarried status as an affir-
mation of her womanhood (Derbyshire 355; N. Friedman 76–77).
They describe the painter, much as early biographers have characterized Woolf herself, as a woman who fears her own sexuality. She
remains a "spinster" (Daiches 84; N. Friedman 64), whom men have
rejected as unmarriageable because of her supposedly awkward
behavior and, in these critics' minds, her implied unattractiveness
(Derbyshire 355). Lily's exclamations of love for Mrs. Ramsay, if
they are mentioned at all in these essays, are explained as merely one
of the many "fixations" plaguing the novel's overly sensitive characters (Troy 87).

Lilienfeld's bold reading of Lily—in which the surrogate daughter
longs "to have this woman, in all her beauty and its meaning, hers
and hers alone" (349) to such an intensity that "[s]he wants her body
to be the one to mingle with that of Mrs. Ramsay" (354)—sets the
stage for lesbian feminist analyses of Lily and Mrs. Ramsay that
follow two decades later (see, also, Marcus, "Taking" 141). Although
Donna Risolo identifies Mrs. Ramsay as "lesbian" (238), most
lesbian feminist interpretations of *To the Lighthouse* focus attention
primarily on Lily. Lise Weil claims that the novel is one of Woolf's
"most radically lesbian texts" (241) in that the reader comes to see the
world through a lesbian feminist lens made possible by Lily Briscoe's

own "perceptual shift" accomplished during her "passage out of patriarchal realism and into a lesbian field of vision" (245). Diana Swanson argues more broadly that "*To the Lighthouse* is inhabited by desiring daughters who wish for something other than the heterosexual, patriarchal domesticity they see their mother living out" (38–39). According to Swanson, although Lily "embodies lesbian knowing and lesbian desire," Cam is also "implicitly lesbian" in her wildness and her resistance to her mother's attempts at "domestication" (40, 41). Highlighting a connection between *To the Lighthouse* and Woolf's lesbian-erotic short story "Moments of Being: 'Slater's Pins Have No Points,'" Annette Oxindine turns her attention to "a strange, unspoken intimacy between Minta Doyle and Nancy Ramsay," which sparks an epiphany in Nancy (56). With the aid of an earlier draft of the novel, Oxindine persuasively pieces together a nascent "transitory homoerotic alliance between" these minor characters, which Woolf muted in the published version (56). Contesting those earlier readings that label Lily an "old maid" (N. Friedman 73) for failing to win the heart of even the lonely widower William Bankes, Ruth Vanita convincingly demonstrates that in fact "the homoerotically inclined Lily and Bankes, pitied by the Ramsays, are able to reveal their buried selves to each other" and "develop a lifelong alliance" based on their shared outsider status (175, 176).

LILY BRISCOE'S PAINTING AND WOOLF'S AESTHETIC

Like Woolf, whose intellectual circle included what we would today refer to as "queer" (that is, sexually non-conforming) artists and thinkers, Lily finds lifelong companionship with William Bankes and, later, intellectual camaraderie with Augustus Carmichael (Vanita 165–70, 176–78). However, it is Lily's status as a female artist and the aesthetic sensibility guiding her to complete her painting that critics consider to be the most purposeful yet multivalent parallel between *To the Lighthouse*'s protagonist and its author. From the novel's first publication, critics have sought to identify the specific aesthetic principles Lily follows as she paints Mrs. Ramsay. Many scholars link Lily's aesthetic to either Roger Fry or Vanessa Bell, or to some combination—or refashioning—of their Post-Impressionist ideals and practices: formalism, abstraction, domestic subjects, the supremacy of art (see, for example, Roberts, "Vision"; Goring; Gillespie, *Sisters'*; Goldman, *Feminist*; Tickner). Masami Usui connects

Lily's aesthetic to two women, Emily Carr and Frances Hodgkins, of the St. Ives school of painting during the first decades of the twentieth century. Beyond visual art and art theory, however, commentators also connect Lily's artistic perspective, as well as Woolf's own as realized in the novel, to the insights of numerous early-twentieth-century thinkers, including philosophers Henri-Louis Bergson and Bertrand Russell and physicists Albert Einstein and David Bohm (see, for example, Kumar; Banfield, "Time Passes"; Donaldson; Stockton; Hussey, "*To the Lighthouse* and Physics").

As the list of influences on and parallels between Woolf's method in *To the Lighthouse* and innovations in twentieth-century thought is inexhaustible, I will focus on a few salient interpretations of Lily's painting from scholarship published in the last twenty-five years. By the phrase "Lily's painting," I mean to draw attention to both her process of painting and the object she creates. In *The Sisters' Arts: The Writing and Painting of Virginia Woolf and Vanessa Bell* (1988), the most comprehensive study to date of the intersection between Vanessa Bell's and Virginia Woolf's aesthetics, Diane Filby Gillespie sketches the web of meta-textual elements encasing Lily's painting. She comments: "Woolf creates a portrait of Lily Briscoe creating a portrait, however abstract, of Mrs. Ramsay, but she creates her own portrait of Mrs. Ramsay and her own partial self-portrait besides" (222). Underscoring meta-textuality, Paul Goring explains how Lily's painting functions as a laden symbol within the novel, specifically "a reading of the text within the text. Her picture functions as a supposed literal visualization of the novel's form, a concrete realization of what Virginia Woolf believes the reader constructs mentally" (222).

Not surprisingly, critics continue to disagree about what Lily's painting shows the reader, both literally—what the painting looks like—and figuratively—what it signifies in terms of the novel's meaning. For instance, Thomas Matro contests readings of Lily's painting and Woolf's novel that argue either that the book endorses the supremacy of art over life, that is, interpersonal relations, or, similarly, that unity is finally achieved through aesthetic formalism when Lily completes her painting. He posits instead that Woolf transforms Roger Fry's aesthetic formalism into "a major ironic theme showing human relations and aesthetic relations to be remarkably similar and similarly unsatisfactory" (212). Framing her interpretation of the novel in terms of the author's reinterpreting her own memories of a family's history, Christine Froula attends to Woolf's rewriting of "the traditional quest romance" in *To the Lighthouse* both from the perspective of the female subject and through the lens of modernist abstraction (130). In "seek[ing] a truth behind appearance" (Froula 149), Lily and Woolf discover "the everyday world of things in themselves" (165) at the present moment, at last separated from their Victorian parental figures; their quest leads to a "dawning recognition that what she desires she already possesses" (166).

Although the novel obscures what Lily creates on her canvas—the exact details of the painting's subject, colors, shapes, and chiaroscuro—critics use what little information Woolf provides to reach myriad conclusions. Jane de Gay sees the purple "triangular shape" as Woolf's inversion of Madonna iconography venerating the Virgin Mary in Renaissance painting (6–7), which Woolf's great Aunt, Julia Margaret Cameron, also reworked in her Victorian photographs (10–11). The line down the center of Lily's painting, according to de Gay, represents the "precarious balance" between the contradiction of both reverencing and rejecting the mother figure (21). Translating into French feminist terminology the contradictory nature of Lily's position vis à vis the mother figure, Mary Jacobus interprets this central line multiply: it represents the "imaginary plentitude of the phallic mother" that the child, within psychoanalytic theory, imagines so as to veil her sense of deprivation from her own phallic lack; or, it is "the line of minimal difference that makes possible the process . . . [of] emergence of the subject as distinct from the mother . . ." (93–94). Thus, "the price Lily pays for finishing her picture is the casting out of the mother" (Jacobus 109), but through it she gains her subjectivity.

WAR, NATION, EMPIRE

If *To the Lighthouse* maps Woolf's psychic battle to mourn the loss of her mother while evoking her presence through the creation of art, then, as Tammy Clewell explains, that process is inextricably tied to the material warfare plaguing a nation. For Clewell detects, as does Matro, "a certain irony in Woolf's depiction of art as an aesthetic remedy for the painful experience of loss" (218). According to her, the line in the center of Lily's final painting both "recalls the way 'Time Passes' separates the novel's own prewar and postwar sections" and, analogously, "distinguishes a time characterized by Mrs. Ramsay's presence and another by her absence. . . . That Lily conveys both absence and presence in the space of a single canvas does not suggest the attainment of a mythic unity typically associated with modernist aesthetics, but rather . . . allows the loss of Mrs. Ramsay and prewar cultural values to inform present understanding" (218).

Just as we have seen scholarship on *To the Lighthouse* make a case for aesthetic unity and familial harmony, on the one hand, and unresolved and irreconcilable contradictions, on the other, so too do the critical responses to color in the novel reflect a tension between admixture into a new ideal and transformation that maintains differences. Jack Stewart, drawing from chromatics and optics as well as the specific use of color by Post-Impressionist painters such as Paul Cézanne, aptly emphasizes that "color/character associations are not reducible to one-to-one symbolic equations" (439) in *To the Lighthouse*. Instead, "each character modifies and is modified by a complex 'system of relations'—involving virtual color, mass, and line— . . . " (Stewart 455). As a mixture of red and blue hues, or, more accurately, a "[m]erging [of] opposite ends of the spectrum," purple, as in Lily's purple triangle, becomes "a direct sign of integration" (Stewart 449; see, also, 447, 453).

However, as with many feminist scholars writing since the 1970s, but particularly those of the past decade, Jane Goldman resists any reading of *To the Lighthouse* that perceives the seamless "integration" of masculinity and the maternal feminine to be part of Lily's final aesthetic vision. Instead, Goldman theorizes what she calls a "feminist prismatics" (*Feminist* 208) of color toward which the novel and Lily's painterly practice move. In *The Feminist Aesthetics of Virginia Woolf: Modernism, Post-Impressionism, and the Politics of the Visual* (1998), Goldman offers an ingenious reading of color symbolism and chiaroscuro in *To the Lighthouse* against the larger contexts of Vanessa Bell's English Post-Impressionist paintings and the British suffrage movement's creation and use of visual art. The colors of "red, white, and blue of a Union Jack" visible in the novel's opening "vignette of family values, implicitly connected (in the image of the Army and Navy catalogue and in Mrs Ramsay's [sic] ambitions for her son) with imperialism and colonialism" (Goldman, *Feminist* 171), give way at various moments to glimpses of the whites, greens, and purples of the early-twentieth-century British suffrage movement and its colorful protest banners (172, 173, 177, 179). The central line Lily paints, Goldman argues, "suggests the feminist reclamation of the first person," which "contests and transforms" the enlightenment "I" of male subjectivity epitomized through Mr. Ramsay in the novel's opening (*Feminist* 185).

Goldman's referencing the British flag and the relationship of nationalism and imperialism to the ideologies of the English middle-class family illustrates a move within Virginia Woolf scholarship, and literary criticism more generally, known as "postcolonial" and "transnational" studies. Numerous Woolf critics, following Jane Marcus's lead in her essay "Britannia Rules *The Waves*" (1992), have analyzed *To the Lighthouse* from either postcolonial or transnational perspectives. The former considers how the institution of British imperialism and its effects are born out in literature during and after formal colonial rule. The latter addresses "*the shuttling activity through which nations have emerged under the episteme of modernity/ coloniality and as reproduced by its racial and sexual ordering*" (Doyle, "Transnational" 533; see, also, Sarker).

For example, Heidi Stalla offers a fascinating link between Woolf's character of William Bankes in *To the Lighthouse* and the historical personage of the same name—the nineteenth-century Member of Parliament for Cambridge University, friend of Byron, and part-time explorer, the "'Traveller in the East'" (22). Tracing the imperial exploits of this amateur Egyptologist as well as the numerous references to Egyptian people and objects in Woolf's novel, Stalla offers a tentative, yet compelling, argument: "Considering the patriarchal theme running through *To the Lighthouse* . . . I want to suggest that the choice of name for William Bankes . . . does two things. It playfully alludes to one of the most legendary tyrants in history, the ancient Egyptian pharaoh Ramses II, and it recalls the age of exploration, discovery, and imperialism that established England's patriarchal authority in the East" (22).

In my own scholarship, I use the early juxtaposition of Mrs. Ramsay and Queen Victoria's portrait in *To the Lighthouse* as an allegory about Britain's imperial conquest, through which I read the rest of the novel. Although this imperial narrative parallels the feminist tale about a modern woman resisting the Victorian marriage imperative, the stories interconnect and sustain one another. Guiding her students to connect the imperial to the domestic by introducing Antonio Gramsci's concept of "hegemony," Jeanette McVicker, in an essay on teaching *To the Lighthouse*, explains how in the novel, as in everyday life, "the institutions that make up society—the family, the academy, art and culture, the government—all perpetuate ideology, working together, as a continuum, to promote the 'truths' a nation asserts" ("Reading" 100). Neither any of Woolf's characters, nor the author herself, escapes "the demands of power exerted at various sites in the imperial continuum . . ." (McVicker, "Reading" 104). The postcolonial perspective, then, both makes visible the subtle subtext of imperialist contest embedded within the domestic narrative of conflict and illuminates how these stories of adventure and hearth, when viewed within the wider contexts of Enlightenment thinking and Western aesthetics, inextricably interweave throughout Woolf's novel. Susan Stanford Friedman cogently articulates the presence of geopolitics in *To the Lighthouse* this way: "the domestic and the foreign . . . are co-complicit and interpenetrating. . . . Patriarchal folly at home is both a cause and a reflection of militarist and nationalist folly abroad. And vice versa" (121, 125).

Focusing centrally on Woolf's construction of Lily Briscoe in relation to European notions of "otherness," Mary Lou Emery, Urmila Seshagiri, and Laura Doyle demonstrate how the feminist anti-imperialist implications of *To the Lighthouse* do not merely co-exist with but rather actually depend upon sexological, Orientalist, and racialist discourses that posit an abject "other" and objectified "others" who unwittingly enable Lily to emerge as *To the Lighthouse*'s new central normative subject. The character of Mrs. McNab in "Time Passes" is one such "other." By analyzing Mrs. McNab's function and figuration in the novel in light of turn-of-the-century pseudo-scientific writings on human sexuality that conflate European women, indigenous and other colonized peoples, and the English working classes, Mary Lou Emery demonstrates how "Mrs. McNab as stereotype is not a character but a process of subject-positioning. She 'works' structurally at the center of the novel to reposition an ideological dichotomy of private and public so that a new female subject may be negotiated in contest but also in compromise with dominant representations of women's 'nature'" (Emery 233).

Urmila Seshagiri exposes and historicizes the racialized language and appropriations in *To the Lighthouse* by contextualizing them within histories of Bloomsbury antics and modernist aesthetics, which looked to so-called "primitive" art for inspiration to remake itself. She argues that "the novel's representations of race—literal and metaphorical, historical and ahistorical—lie at the heart of its artistic experimentation and its political subversions" (66). In the most nuanced and insightful interpretation of Lily's "Chinese eyes" to date, Seshagiri asserts that "the encrypted foreignness of Lily Briscoe's 'little Chinese eyes' first forces Lily's sexual devaluation and subsequently enables her artistic freedom. Racial difference, in other words, provides a meeting ground for social critique and aesthetic innovation in *To the Lighthouse*. . . . Woolf uses Lily's 'Chinese eyes' to effect the transition between Lily the 'skimpy old maid' and Lily the accomplished artist" (75). Racial alterity works in this novel to "exclude her socially [from patriarchal demands upon white, middle-class women] *and* elevate her artistically" via appropriating non-European aesthetic traditions (Seshagiri 67). Emery and Seshagiri, by examining the characters of Mrs. McNab and Lily Briscoe, respectively, illumine Woolf's indebtedness to discourses of class, colonial, and racial differences to accomplish her aesthetic and political objectives—the middle-class Englishwoman's new subjecthood as liberated modern artist at the expense of the "others," whose voices the novel mutes.

By contrast, Laura Doyle, in "Voyaging Beyond the Race Mother: *Melymbrosia* and *To the Lighthouse*," sees Mrs. McNab, an Irish working-class woman, as essential to the novel's critique of "the sustaining colonialism" that underpins the English middle-class Victorian family. "What Mrs. McNab sees in the mirror deflates the aggrandizing hopes of those [in "Time Passes"] who go alone to the sea in search of final answers as well as those who imagine ideal marriages between men and women. . . . With Mrs. Ramsay gone, the other mother's labor behind her labor becomes visible, unembellished, in the mirror" (167). Doyle considers though ultimately rejects the contention that Woolf appropriates the working-class cum colonial subject's labor in order to aggrandize the middle-class Englishwoman artist, Lily Briscoe, a substitute for Woolf herself (168). She contends instead that through the strategic use of irony and the narrator's greater identification with Mrs. McNab, the novel "dethrones" and "moves finally beyond all mother figures" to usher in a "shared agency among narrator, middle-class English 'daughters,' and non-English working-class women" and a newly politicized art (168, 170).

The tension—within Woolf's own writing and among critics' differing conclusions about that writing—between Woolf's feminist anti-imperialist critique and her recuperation of racist and classist tropes to uphold the female artist as the premier agent of progressive social change has fueled fierce debate among Woolf scholars.

(For biographical and historical information about Woolf's relationship with her real-life servants, see Light 200–03, 216–19; see, also, MacKay 241–42.)

POSTSTRUCTURALISM AND BEYOND

Characteristic of most contemporary interpretations of the novel, including many discussed above, Gayatri Spivak's reading of *To the Lighthouse*, "Unmaking and Making in *To the Lighthouse*" (1988), cannot be pigeon-holed into one critical category. It combines deconstruction, feminism, postcolonialism, biographical criticism, lesbian reading, and psychoanalysis. Spivak argues that the novel can be read as an "allegory of a reason menaced by madness, an ontology on the brink of disaster by the near-uncoupling of the copula" that occurs in "Time Passes" (38). Specifically, she interprets the novel, with its two major sections, "The Window" and "The Lighthouse," connected through the corridor of "Time Passes," through its structural resemblance to the "copula" (30–31), a term from grammar and logic for the verb form of "to be" or "to seem" used to link a sentence's subject with its predicate. As the Latin root for the word "copulation," the concept of the "copula" allows Spivak to read *To the Lighthouse* as a story about the struggle over textual and thus ontological meaning as it is shaped by sexual politics. Spivak's deconstructionist approach takes as its starting assumption the "limits of language" (38): that is, language, and artifacts made up of language, can neither stabilize identity nor construct logical ways of "being" because, as with Western logic, it produces meaning through differences between terms in a closed system of signification rather than by legitimate recourse to any absolute truth or presence. According to Spivak, *To the Lighthouse* is not about the desire for androgyny, the need to bring together the oppositions represented by Mr. and Mrs. Ramsay (40, 42, 43). Rather, the novel maps both Woolf's and Lily's attempts "to construct the copula, however precarious, of art"—to create "a woman's vision of a woman"—"by using a man [Mr. Ramsay] as an instrument" to do so (45). *To the Lighthouse*, Spivak provocatively concludes, stages the workings of "womb-envy" (43–45) (as opposed to "penis envy," Freud's theory that women envy the male penis as a source of sexual pleasure and social power). The novel accomplishes this by articulating a story about "the womb . . . not [as] an emptiness or a mystery, . . . [but rather as] a place of production" (45). Although tangential to her central argument, Spivak links the "erotic textuality" (40) implicit in *To the Lighthouse* to Woolf's intense and eroticized love for her sister, Vanessa Bell (40, 42). (See Lee for further discussion of this subject.)

This relatively brief and necessarily incomplete sampling of the richly varied critiques of *To the Lighthouse* over the past eighty-some years is intended as an invitation to engage in further reading, rather than a claim to represent the whole. As Mark Hussey describes in his 2005 introduction to the novel, "[m]ore has been written about *To the Lighthouse* than about any of Woolf's other books" (lxv). In chapter 6, I offer specific suggestions of readings to expand one's critical perspective on the novel.

CHAPTER 5

ADAPTATION, INTERPRETATION
AND INFLUENCE

A writer's country is a territory within his own brain; and we run the risk of disillusionment if we try to turn such phantom cities into tangible brick and mortar. [. . .] In the same way too the great dead come to each of us in their own guise, and their image is more palpable and enduring than any shapes of flesh and blood.
—*Virginia Woolf, "Literary Geography," 1905,* Essays *1*

Any attempt to dramatise a famous novel is perilous. Readers build pictures of characters, places and events in their heads while they read. Any alternative representation presents them with a different picture that can often disappoint. And Woolf's novel poses more obstacles than most when it comes to transposing it to the theatre.
—*Katie Mitchell, director of* Waves, *2006*

WOOLF IN POPULAR CULTURE

In "Literary Geography," a review of two books about the literary landscapes of William Makepeace Thackeray and Charles Dickens, Virginia Woolf warns readers to tread lightly when assessing artistic influence. She asks one to consider an author's connection to "the great dead" (35) as a highly personal imaginary relationship rather than a literal one born of actual acquaintance or familiarity with a person's biography. Woolf decries the type of literary interpretation that diminishes the work of the imagination to a calculus of external influences, whether biographical or geographical. We might consider Woolf's warning about tracing influences as we embark on an exploration of *To the Lighthouse*'s influence on subsequent works of the imagination. Even adaptations of the novel, the central focus of this chapter, are, concomitantly, themselves new works of art. And yet, art bearing the same name as an earlier creation begs comparison to the original. In truth, such art is simultaneously a new creation and an interpretation.

With the commercial and critical success of Stephen Daldry's star-studded feature film *The Hours* (2002), based on the 1998 Michael Cunningham novel of the same name, Virginia Woolf's own status as one of "the great dead" has been secured in the twenty-first-century popular imagination. After the film's release, "common reader[s]" in the United States eagerly snapped up Woolf's much praised novel *Mrs. Dalloway* (1925), the source of inspiration for Cunningham's work, making *Mrs. Dalloway* a *New York Times* best-seller in 2003. Yet, even before *The Hours* made Woolf a household name for something other than the title of Edward Albee's 1962 play, *Whose Afraid of Virginia Woolf?*, Sally Potter's feature film *Orlando* (1992), based on Woolf's 1928 gender-bending fictional "love letter" (Nicolson, *Portrait* 202) to Vita Sackville-West, became an overnight sensation, establishing Woolf's "hipster" credentials with art house movie denizens. Another successful film based on a Woolf novel followed a few years later, Oscar-winning Dutch filmmaker Marlene Gorris's *Mrs. Dalloway* (1997). Then in October 2006 at the National Theatre in London, Woolf's most experimental novel *The Waves* (1931), which the author considered to "embody, at last, the exact shapes my brain holds" (V. Woolf, *Diary* 4: 53), was transmuted into theatrical performance in Katie Mitchell's *Waves*. The highly experimental multimedia production received rave reviews and has since toured internationally in 2008, including a 10-day run in New York City as part of Lincoln Center's "Great Performers" 2008–09 season.

What does all this box office attention to *Mrs. Dalloway*, *Orlando*, and *The Waves*, not to mention Eileen Atkins's one-woman stage production in 1989 of *A Room of One's Own*, mean for *To the Light-house*, Woolf's most acclaimed novel? *Slant Magazine* film reviewer Ed Gonzalez rumors that *Hours* author Michael Cunningham is vying to rewrite *To the Lighthouse,* Cunningham's favorite of Woolf's fiction—as a refashioned novel or screenplay, Gonzalez does not say. In fact, *To the Lighthouse* has already been popularized in the late twentieth and early twenty-first centuries through Woolf-inspired visual art, dance, screen and stage adaptations, and literary homages. From Judy Chicago's 1974–79 *The Dinner Party* art installation with its Virginia Woolf place setting featuring a tabletop runner adorned with a stitched and airbrushed lighthouse beam, to Colin Gregg's 1983 BBC television movie based on the book, to Jeanette Winterson's 2006 novel *Lighthousekeeping*, to the Stephen Pelton Dance Theater's 2009 contemporary dance work *it was this: it was this:*, exploring Woolf's use of punctuation in a paragraph of the novel (Maggio), *To the Lighthouse* continues to be remade and revisioned in myriad forms, on different scales, and with varying degrees of success.

This chapter will explore in depth three examples of the novel's refashioning: Australian artist Suzanne Bellamy's triptych painting *To the Lighthouse* (1999), Northern California sculptor Marilyn Andrews's multimedia installation *To the Lighthouse* (2008), and the Berkeley Repertory Theatre's 2007 world premiere of *To the Lighthouse* based on the play by Adele Edling Shank. Unlike Winterson's arresting novel, which pays homage to *To the Lighthouse*'s formal experimentation and central symbol and motifs but presents an entirely different story, Bellamy's, Andrews's, and Shank's art aims to interpret Woolf's original work by transposing it to a new medium. I will first say a few words about the aforementioned BBC film, however, as it is the adaptation to which readers are most apt to turn.

FILM ADAPTATION

Katie Mitchell's words in the epigraph describing her decision to turn an avant-garde novel by a beloved author into equally bold performance art underscore the fact that fidelity to the original, or at least to any given reader's interpretation of that material, colors responses to the indebted piece. This dilemma applies to the film as well. Reviewing the first U.S. airing on the Public Broadcasting Station of the BBC-1 film *To the Lighthouse*, *New York Times* television critic John J. O'Connor writes in 1984 that "Hugh Stoddart's extremely sensitive and illuminating" screenplay under Colin Gregg's direction engenders a production that "is very special indeed" (C33). O'Connor's enthusiastic response to the 115-minute film is representative of the reviews the picture received in its day. Starring Kenneth Branagh as Charles Tansley and Rosemary Harris as Mrs. Ramsay,

To the Lighthouse was nominated for a British Film and Television Arts award (BAFTA) for best "single drama" in television in 1983.

The film has not aged well, however. Twenty-five years after its release, it strikes one, this viewer at least, as a meandering story about a verbally abusive father and husband, who assuages his disappointments in life, particularly those stemming from his professional failures, by serving as guest of honor at the awards ceremony for the annual wrestling tournament hosted by the local Cornish. The setting is Cornwall, not the Hebrides; the number of characters is reduced. Augustus Carmichael and Prue Ramsay do double duty, fulfilling, respectively, William Bankes's and Minta Doyle's roles as well as their own. Mrs. McNab is eliminated. It is not the liberties taken with the novel's setting, scenes, and characters that cause the film to fall short although the addition of the outdoor wrestling match lends itself to D. H. Lawrence's fiction, not Woolf's. Rather, the film lacks longevity because it renders neither the characters nor the ideas underpinning them complexly. The gloomy almost flat visuals throughout much of the movie, the overpowering yet dreary musical score, and the historically accurate mise en scène only compound the problem by reducing the work to a predictable and dull period piece.

The few moments of dramatic tension in the film originate with the wrestling match, Mr. Ramsay's rages, and Mrs. Ramsay's fainting in the garden, a scene added to foreshadow her death. Although the dinner party and the lighthouse expedition remain, these scenes lack the subtlety and import of their originals. Most significantly, Lily Briscoe recedes to the margins of this composition. She appears but is barely recognizable. Dour and self-deprecating, Lily voices hackneyed feminist phrases throughout the film while painting pictures in the style of Hallmark greeting cards, not Post-Impressionist art. Despite sporting bobbed hair and a flapper headband in the final scenes, Lily offers a grim alternative to the browbeaten Mrs. Ramsay.

Although I have, on occasion, shown a scene from the film in class to help students concretize the basic storyline, characters, and setting of the novel, many professors who teach *To the Lighthouse* avoid incorporating the film into their lesson plans altogether. As one instructor advises fellow teachers, "'Whatever you do, don't use the god-awful BBC version of *To the Lighthouse*! It betrays the material, adding things like a wrestling match, and generally ruins the book'" (qtd. in Daugherty and Pringle 20).

VISUAL ART INSPIRED BY *TO THE LIGHTHOUSE*

Visual art inspired by a novel is less apt to rankle its readers. Of the artwork created as a tribute to *To the Lighthouse*, Vanessa Bell's book jacket design and her tiled fireplace surround are the most famous examples—although one should keep in mind Frances Spalding's assertion that Bell's large painting *The Nursery* (1930–32) may have been inspired by Woolf's fictionalized reflection on their childhood as well (251). As with all of her book jackets for the Hogarth Press, Bell had "not read a word of the book" her sister had written before creating the design that would adorn the finished publication (V. Bell qtd. in Lehmann 27). As Diane Filby Gillespie observes of Bell's book jacket designs generally, "the tensions emerge from black juxta-posed with white, color, or the floral motif, and from recognizable images combined with abstract arrangements of lines, shapes, and colors. . . . [T]he jacket designs are often pleasing by themselves. Looked at with each other and with the texts, though, the covers evoke the psychological oppositions which so fascinated Virginia Woolf" (*Sisters'* 266). The pleasing nature of the designs is, perhaps, born out by the availability of reproductions of *Mrs. Dalloway*'s and *To the Lighthouse*'s covers as 59 x 84 cm posters, available from the online store POPARTUK beginning at £9.95.

Bell's design for *To the Lighthouse*'s book jacket features an abstracted yet recognizable lighthouse in the center surrounded by a decorative scalloped frame. The black and off-white design, accented with pale blue, is striking for the movement and energy it evokes by way of the bold waves at the lighthouse's base and the expansive triangular halo of light suggested at its crown. Biographer Julia Briggs remarks that Vanessa's design "perfectly captur[es] the 'fountain of joy' experienced by Cam and Mrs. Ramsay in the novel" (*Virginia Woolf* 184). The use of negative space in the application of black color to demarcate a frame, which is solid at the top of the page and pointillistic and narrow at the bottom, creates the dual effect of darkness and light, night and day, surrounding the central lighthouse image. Writing to her sister after having received the cover for the U.S. edition, Woolf remarks that she "thought it lovely—. [. . .] Your style is unique; because so truthful; and therefore it upsets one completely" (*Letters* 3: 391).

Three years later in 1930, Bell painted abstract shapes and a central tableau of a lighthouse and sailboat out at sea on a tiled fireplace surround in Woolf's bedroom at Monks House, Rodmell, Sussex (see Gillespie, *Sisters'* 158 for a black and white photographic reproduction). Jeanette Winterson, who visited Monks House in search of traces of the great writer, declares of Bell's handiwork, "It can only be a recognition of one of Virginia's best books," not an illustration ("Virginia Woolf" 464). For Diane Gillespie, the triangular shape of the boat's sail alludes to the "triangular purple shape" of Mrs. Ramsay's essence in her sister's novel; the tableau's vertical lines—the sailboat's mast, the lighthouse, and the lighthouse beam's reflection in the water—mirror the final line of Lily Briscoe's painting at the novel's conclusion (*Sisters'* 157–58). The remaining tiles contain circles, oblongs, triangles, and squares sparsely painted on a white background in light blue, green, brown, and gold in the decorative style of the Omega Workshops.

Many visual artists working today continue to be inspired by Virginia Woolf's writings, especially *To the Lighthouse* with its protagonist painter, Lily Briscoe. In the United States, for example, retired teacher and artist Isota Tucker Epes's *Two Ways of Seeing* and Woolf scholar Elisa Kay Sparks's computer-generated *Vision Statement* (1996) evoke *To the Lighthouse*—the former, by portraying a conversation between two female artists at the easel; the latter, by collaging together images from the novel and Woolf's life into a dizzying vortex. In Epes's and Sparks's *To the Lighthouse* pieces, Virginia Woolf appears both as herself and as the "triangular purple shape" Lily imagines Mrs. Ramsay's essence to be (V. Woolf, *To the Lighthouse* 52).

Yet, it is Australian sculptor, painter, and printmaker Suzanne Bellamy, former historian turned Woolf scholar and artist, who has created the most extensive archive of Woolf-inspired images of any studio artist working today. Bellamy, who describes herself as a lesbian artist, characterizes her relationship to Virginia Woolf as both a "love affair" and a "creative partnership" ("Pattern" 23). She notes that "[w]hen I first began to read Virginia Woolf's novels, I felt she wrote like a sculptor. She was able with words to build forms, strip away surfaces, shed representation in a way different from abstraction" ("Pattern" 32). After decades of reading Virginia Woolf, whose work she regards as "intentionally visual in its core structure" ("Artist's Statement"), Bellamy devoted six years to work full-time on her Virginia Woolf project, which combines paintings, prints, and a three-dimensional installation piece entitled *Woolfworld* (2002).

Part of this project, Bellamy's *To the Lighthouse* triptych painting (1999), which she undertook independently yet in concert with Tucker Epes (Bellamy, "Painting" 245), replicates the novel's three-part structure. Bellamy explains, in her essay "'Painting the Words': A Version of Lily Briscoe's Paintings from *To the Lighthouse*," that from the moment she began to conceive of this piece, she envisioned it being oriented vertically rather than horizontally, which she likens to "a Chinese road painting" rather than a Western landscape (248–49). The triptych recalls Bell's fireplace surround in its use of color, particularly its blues and umbers, and its combination of picturesque seascape and elemental shapes. Bellamy's work, however, uses both representational elements and abstract forms to convey the metaphysical journey the novel plots in three movements—from structures of domesticity and the family to a "dark night of the soul" to the harmonizing of landscape, spiritual essences, and occupations.

The first panel depicts a tall white house overlooking the sea. An orange sun hovers over it, and in the distance a sailboat, indicated by an orange triangle, and a lighthouse are barely visible. In between the house and its counterpart, a white wall adorned with purple flowers, stands a pear tree with an upside-down kitchen table balanced on its branches, a reference to Andrew's explanation of Mr. Ramsay's philosophical studies (V. Woolf, *To the Lighthouse* 23, 25; see Bellamy, "Painting" 247). The viewer's eye is drawn to the house's large open window where a chair and two figures appear: one figure is small, brown, and rounded; the other, large, triangular, and purple—presumably James and Mrs. Ramsay.

In the third panel, a view at close range, the window is all that is visible of the house. The pear tree's outstretched branches no longer contain a kitchen table but instead appear to bridge the white space framed by the window and the white space of the now empty wall—or is it a canvas? (see Bellamy, "Painting" 249). The triangular purple shape has left its perch by the window, and it has grown bigger and multiplied. Purple and lavender triangles float away from the house toward the lighthouse and, along with two orange triangles, toward the white sun.

In describing her process to create this piece, Bellamy emphasizes the fact that she "did not want to illustrate the novel, I wanted to take Lily's journey in paint" ("Painting" 245). Nonetheless, more so than many of her subsequent works, such as *The Waves* (2000), the luminous *Water* (2003), *Woolf's London* (2002), and *Seeing Through a Film of Yellow* (2002), a reference to a line from Woolf's unfinished memoir, "A Sketch of the Past," *To the Lighthouse* incorporates so many iconic elements from Woolf's novel that it is difficult not to respond to it as illustration, the first and third panels, particularly.

The second panel, an abstract nightscape, reduces most of the representational elements of the other panels to form, texture, and color: black, white, gray, purple, and red (see Bellamy, "Painting" 246–47). The remaining recognizable element, the window, appears closed and confining. The outlines of the full, yet fully eclipsed, moon resting above the curved shoreline with its spit of land suggest yin yang, shapes present in the other two panels as well. Bellamy explains that initially she had envisioned the "Time Passes" panel as an "eclipse"— signaling loss and death (246). "Then my reading and seeing brought a different source of light to the foreground. It was not all black, it was not absence, it was not dark. My painting began to glow like a dark jewel. . . . I was seeing a densely alive void between states of ordinary perception" (246–47). Indeed, this central panel is the most visually striking of the three—due, in part, to its lack of representational elements and its reliance on texture, color, and form.

By creating art in response to Woolf's writing, Bellamy hopes that "Virginia Woolf can stay alive while I and others still find points of dynamic exchange with her" ("Pattern" 28). One of those "others" is California metal artist Marilyn Andrews. Andrews has recently completed a series of provocative sculptures, composed of bronze, fabric, glass, and other materials, based on *To the Lighthouse*. Austere abstractions of fictional elements, these robust pieces arrest the senses with their bold lines and occasional whimsical adornments. *Lily Briscoe's Painting,* for example, embodies the formal precision of Lily Briscoe's aesthetic combined with the rigor the artist must undergo to transmute her vision into material composition. There are two versions of this piece: one bronze, suede, and fabric, and the other made entirely of metals. Both feature a blank or nearly blank canvas supported by an easel. Of the piece composed entirely of metals, an aquamarine patina cutout of aluminum overlaid on the bottom quarter of the canvas creates the appearance of waves. This cutout echoes the scalloped frame of Vanessa Bell's book jacket design as well as suggests, through its use of negative space, a row of triangles diving into the sea. The piece concretizes "the problem of space" (V. Woolf, *To the Lighthouse* 171) that defines Lily's, and presumably Woolf's, aesthetic project: "Beautiful and bright it should be on the surface, feathery and evanescent, one color melting into another like the colors on a butterfly's wing; but beneath the fabric must be clamped together with bolts of iron" (V. Woolf, *To the Lighthouse* 171). In Andrews's sculptures, we literally see these bolts. *Mrs. Ramsay's Knitting* playfully combines thick bronze bolts in place of knitting needles sunk into a fiberglass bowl filled with undyed shredded wood, known as excelsior. The title of the piece alludes to Mrs. Ramsay's knitting a stocking for the lighthouse keeper's son. The sculpture itself resembles a wok filled with noodles and whimsically suggests the matriarch's role as domestic goddess, who is equally adept at fabricating garments, overseeing the kitchen staff, and generally knitting the family together in harmony.

TO THE LIGHTHOUSE IN PERFORMANCE

In 1999, literary critic Stephen Putzel proclaimed that "[n]o Woolf novel has been adapted to film, theater, or performance art more often than has *Orlando*. The colorful romp through four centuries, the sex changes, the scenes set around the world, the narrative voice—all present adapters, producers, designers, directors, and actors with exciting challenges" (450). By contrast, *To the Lighthouse* contains little action, a slight plot, and dramatic tension restricted to the internalized thoughts of its characters. According to at least one theater critic, "a stream-of-consciousness novel is hopelessly unsuited to dramatisation" (Billington 28). Another claims that "[i]f you had to pick a novel harder [than *To the Lighthouse*] for a four-person cast to bring to theatrical life, you would have to scour the world for a better candidate" (Nightingale 12). Despite the obstacles to its dramatization, between the years 1995 and 2007 *To the Lighthouse* has been adapted for live performance for at least three separate productions—two stage productions and one radio play: the Empty Space Theatre Company's 1995 London production directed by Andrew Holmes with a script by Julia Limer, the Shaw Festival Theatre's 2000 Niagara-on-the-Lake, Canada radio production directed by Ann Hodges with a script by Lindsay Bell, and the Berkeley Repertory Theatre's 2007 Berkeley, California production directed by Les Waters with a script by Adele Edling Shank and musical composition by Paul Dresher. My focus for the remainder of this chapter will be the Berkeley Repertory Theatre's production, which I attended on 24 March 2007.

Steven Putzel, in his essay "Virginia Woolf and 'The Distance of the Stage'" (1999), and Lindsay Bell, in "Transmitting the Voices, Voyages and Visions: Adapting Virginia Woolf's *To the Lighthouse* for Radio" (2001), analyze, respectively, the Empty Space Theatre Company's play, which was produced with only four cast members acting in multiple roles, and the Shaw Festival Theatre's radio performance. Most useful for my purposes here, Putzel's and Bell's essays provide insight into "Virginia Woolf's own performance theory" through their careful readings of Woolf's writings on theater (L. Bell 73). As Lindsay Bell explains, "Woolf's responses towards theatre, or more specifically, towards performance, oscillated between attraction and repulsion. Her attraction to the theatre often relied on how closely her own reader's version of the play resembled the play as performed upon the stage" (75; see, also, Putzel 438). Both Putzel and Bell quote from Woolf's essay "Notes on an Elizabethan Play" (1925) to illustrate Woolf's ambivalence about theatrical production, given Woolf's preference for solitary contemplation (Putzel 440) and her penchant for "[s]tream-of-consciousness narratives [which] privilege the mind over the body, and therefore, privilege the mind over action" (L. Bell 79): "There is no privacy here. Always the door opens and some one comes in. All is shared, made visible, audible, dramatic. Meanwhile, as if tired with company, the mind steals off to muse in solitude; to think, not to act; to comment, not to share; to explore its own darkness, not the bright lit-up surfaces of others" (V. Woolf, "Notes" 69). And although Woolf preferred to read plays and so animate them in her own mind to witnessing them in the company of others, brought to life by others, Stephen Putzel reminds us that "Virginia Woolf's work *is* performance—her narrative is dialogic, always engaging readers into co-authorship" (466). He concludes, having studied numerous performance adaptations of several of Woolf's writings, that "[a]dapters who rely on realism, naïve symbolism, or the traditional musical still fail in their attempts to bring Woolf to the stage. It takes the postmodern stage—with its use of mime, dance, opera, contrapuntal music, minimalist sets, and, most of all, its demand of complicity from the audience—to produce a successful performance of Virginia Woolf" (466).

Les Waters's 2007 production of *To the Lighthouse* combines several of these elements—pantomime, light opera, a contemporary musical score, and, although not exactly minimalist, striking experimental set designs as well as elaborate video projections. The play is written in two acts, three scenes each. Although titled variously, four of the play's six scenes are devoted to dramatizing the first section of Woolf's novel, "The Window." The novel's remaining sections, "Time Passes" and "The Lighthouse," are compressed into one scene each. These two scenes are the most experimental of the production, with "Time Passes" narrated primarily through Paul Dresher's musical score, played live by the Seventh Avenue String Quartet, and Jebediah Ike's video montage. Characters noiselessly walk on and off stage miming their parts. In "To the Lighthouse," the play's final scene, the actors alternatively sing and speak their lines.

If we take seriously Putzel's claim above, then the Berkeley Repertory Theatre's production of *To the Lighthouse* ought to have been an unmitigated success. Yet the reviews were mixed. Most major national newspapers, the trade press, and at least one San Francisco-based magazine were on the whole unsympathetic (see, for example, Harvey; Isherwood; Veltman, "A Stage"). Charles Isherwood of the *New York Times* called the play an "awkward and inert attempt" with the adaptation "suffer[ing] from an excess of reverence and a dearth of imaginative license" (B13). Dennis Harvey of the entertainment newspaper *Variety*, apparently not convinced of the play's entertainment value, described the production as a "windy, pretentious bore." By contrast, most local San Francisco, East Bay, and South Bay Area newspaper reviewers lavished praise on at least some elements of the production. Lee Hartgrave of *Beyond Chron*, "San Francisco's Alternative Online Daily," gushed that theatergoers "can actually sense the smell of seawater in the air," so "hypnotic" are the sets and lighting (for more nuanced reviews, see Bullock; Craig; Connema; Jones).

My own response to the Berkeley Repertory Theatre's production of *To the Lighthouse* combines elements from both ends of the critical spectrum. I found the first, third, and fifth scenes, "The Window," "Dinner," and "Time Passes," mesmerizing in their combination of fidelity to Woolf's original and provocative use of sound and visual effects as analogues for complex events and states of being. As did some reviewers, I thought the dinner party scene a triumph in much the same way Woolf believed "[t]he dinner party the best thing I ever wrote: the one thing that I think justifies my faults as a writer" (*Letters* 3: 373). This scene, with its deft juxtaposing of actors speaking their internal thoughts and silently pantomiming polite conversations, does justice to Woolf's novel and to Shank's script, throughout which Woolf's sinuous language is elegantly compressed. It more than made up for the disappointing final scene, "To the Lighthouse," which, although in one sense the most experimental in that many of the lines were sung, was almost lifeless in its presentation and staging. The large wooden sailboat that anchored this scene on stage only added to the sense of stasis—rather than, as called for, transience. The following passage from Woolf's essay "Notes on an Elizabethan Play" encapsulates my overall theater-going experience: "Wandering in the maze of the impossible and tedious story suddenly some passionate intensity seizes us; some sublimity exalts, or some melodious snatch of song enchants. It is a world full of tedium and delight, pleasure and curiosity, of extravagant laughter, poetry, and splendour. But gradually it comes over us, *what then are we being denied?*" (69; emphasis added).

Without knowing anything about the Berkeley Repertory Theatre, one might reasonably assume that these conflicting responses are due to, in Putzel's words, "the postmodern stage['s] . . . demand of complicity from the audience." Given the production's task of satisfying the competing demands made by an esoteric stream-of-consciousness novel and a sophisticated yet entertainment-seeking audience, Les Waters, the production's director as well as the Berkeley Repertory Theatre's Associate Artistic Director, might have felt inclined to tone down the novel's experimentalism in order to make the work engage a range of theatergoers. After all, it was Virginia Woolf who wrote in *A Room of One's Own*, "these webs are not spun in mid-air by incorporeal creatures, but are the work of suffering human beings, and are attached to grossly material things, like [. . .] money" (42). By "webs" she meant the intricacy of Shakespeare's plays and other "extraordinary literature" (41).

Yet this was not the case. In fact the Berkeley Repertory Theatre has a national reputation, and Waters an international one, for risk taking, particularly when it comes to innovations in theatrical form and political iconoclasm ("Press Coverage"). Several of their productions have traveled to New York City's Off-Broadway theaters and achieved national critical acclaim. Obie-winner Waters is considered by many actors and playwrights to be an *artists'* director, attending meticulously to the aesthetic nuances of every piece he directs (Veltman, "Les Waters"; D'Souza, "Press Coverage").

Rather than resulting from too much reverence for the original, as Isherwood posits, the play's unevenness, I believe, stems from how the original was interpreted. As with Woolf's response to theater generally, my satisfaction with the play depended upon how closely the play corresponded to my "own reader's version" of the novel (L. Bell 75). And where Woolf responds to her own question above, "But gradually it comes over us, what then are we being denied?" with, "It is solitude" (69), I rejoin, "It is Lily Briscoe and Mrs. Ramsay's relationship in all its complexity." As was true in the BBC film, in the Berkeley Repertory Theatre's production Lily's intense love for Mrs. Ramsay vanishes from script and stage. Instead, through subtle scripting choices, Lily's friendship with William Bankes assumes romantic proportions beyond Mrs. Ramsay's match-making efforts described in Woolf's novel.

For example, Lily's fantasized moment of intimacy with Mrs. Ramsay—during which she wonders, "Could loving [. . .] make her and Mrs. Ramsay one?" (51)—becomes, in Shank's script, an actual exchange between Lily and Mrs. Ramsay that takes place not in Lily's bedroom, as imagined in the original, but in the nursery. The nursery setting allows Mrs. Ramsay to illustrate to Lily, and presumably the play's audience, "what matters most in this life" as Lily accompanies her to check on her young children, Cam and James. Admittedly, Shank's exposition undercuts this meaning—as "the perfect portrait of childhood innocence she had hoped to show is despoiled" (Shank 57, sc. 4). Nonetheless, this scene in place of Woolf's diminishes the amplitude of the women's relationship and transforms the character of Lily Briscoe. Now instead of "[s]itting on the floor with her arms round Mrs. Ramsay's knees, close as she could get" (V. Woolf, *To the Lighthouse* 50–51), Lily helps Mrs. Ramsay carry out her motherly duties, that is, conceal the boar's skull in order to pacify Cam. Then, once they have exchanged the nursery for the comfort of Mrs. Ramsay's mother's old sofa, Lily laughs and admits, holding Mrs. Ramsay's hand and in response to the woman's insistence that she marry William Bankes, "Sometimes I think so yes, and then I remember how he can't abide it if his potatoes happen to touch his meat" (Shank 59, sc. 4). As Mrs. Ramsay continues to pressure Lily to marry, Lily explains fully her reasons for resisting: "I have my father, I have my home, I have my painting. I like to be alone. I like to be myself. I was not made for all of this"

(Shank 59, sc. 4). These alterations to Woolf's text appear to justify Lily's unmarried status to the audience. By eliminating Lily's desire for Mrs. Ramsay and, to some degree, downplaying her devotion to her art, both central to Woolf's novel, Shank instead characterizes Lily as being too fastidious and reclusive to settle for a marriageable and willing man.

Having interviewed Adele Edling Shank before the production opened, I anticipated that the relationship between Mrs. Ramsay and Lily on stage would avoid any homoerotic underpinnings. For Shank, Woolf's novel does not admit a lesbian subtext. I accepted this outright as the playscript was, after all, neither my nor Woolf's but rather Shank's vision. As Putzel reminds, "Woolf's work . . . is . . . always engaging readers into co-authorship" (466). What surprised me though was Shank's muting of Lily's critique of patriarchy, especially as it operates within the institutions of marriage and family—something unmistakable in and central to Woolf's novel. Without the complexities of Lily and Mrs. Ramsay's bond being developed, even if only in Lily's imagination, the play casts Lily not so much as a necessary observer and critic of the marital and family dynamic but instead as almost incidental to the drama.

One particular moment in the production, presumably included for the purpose of injecting humor, underscores this shift from Woolf's sustained political critique to the play's upholding the status quo. In scene 4, "After Dinner Conversations," just after Mr. Ramsay's attempt to cajole Mrs. Ramsay into saying aloud she loves him, the actor playing Mr. Ramsay, Edmond Genest, stood up, faced the audience, and shook his leg in such a manner as if to signal to the audience the physical lovemaking between the Ramsays that was sure to ensue. During the performance I attended, the audience laughed at the gesture as if on cue. It struck me as not merely gratuitous but rather a deliberate effort to bring the audience together in sympathy. The effect to the play, however, was to undercut further Woolf's radical assessment of society founded on institutionalized heterosexuality and male supremacy.

Another moment in the production that substituted shallow humor for dramatic tension occurred at the end of "Time Passes" (scene 5) when Mrs. McNab, dressed in floor-length charwoman's apparel and in desperate need of a good brassiere, hammed up her performance mopping the floor. Although critics of the novel point to Mrs. McNab as an example of Woolf's own stereotyping of the working class as "witless" and bemoan the changes Woolf made to the holograph draft to diminish her character, her presence in this section of the novel lends itself to multiple and complex interpretations (see, in particular, Emery). By contrast, rather than an elderly woman laboring to beat back the forces of nature and time, the Berkeley Repertory Theatre's portrayal brought to mind Carol Burnett in her signature role as the janitor in her 1967 to 1978 U.S. comedic television variety show *The Carol Burnett Show*.

According to theater scholar Jill Dolan, in *The Feminist Spectator as Critic* (1991), the "theatre creates an ideal spectator carved in the likeness of the dominant culture whose ideology he represents . . ." (1). "Historically, in North American culture, this spectator has been assumed to be white, middle-class, heterosexual, and male" (1). Despite the brilliance of Shank's script, the eloquence of Paul Dresher's original score, the vibrant use of sound and visual effects, and the innovative direction overall, the Berkeley Repertory Theatre's *To the Lighthouse* bowed to convention in its downplaying of Woolf's incisive feminist critique. The result was a diminished experience—for this viewer at least, whose mind at moments wanted to "[steal] off to muse in solitude; [. . .] to explore its own darkness, not the bright lit-up surfaces of others" (V. Woolf, "Notes" 69).

CHAPTER 6

GUIDE TO FURTHER READING

Given the growth of popular interest in Virginia Woolf during the past three decades, as evidenced by numerous feature films and live performances based on her life and writings, it is not surprising that scholarly attention to her work has also exploded. Initial research for chapter 4 of this book, for instance, indicates the following trend: between the years 1942 and 1967 the Modern Language Association's International Bibliography, a central research database for English literature and language studies, listed one or two scholarly essays on *To the Lighthouse* published in English language journals annually. In 1968 the number climbed to three, a 50% increase, and stayed between one and three for the next few years until it shot up to five in 1972 and then eight in 1981. From the 1980s onward, the number steadily rose: 18 in 1984, 21 in 1992, and 36 in 2001 (for some years the figures include essays in edited collections and completed but as yet unpublished Ph.D. dissertations). Although these figures do not reflect all critical responses to the novel, such as chapters in monographs, they do suggest a predicament for students undertaking research or others just wanting to do further reading. Where should one begin?

RECEPTION HISTORY

Readers interested in learning more about the critical reception of *To the Lighthouse* and in identifying additional essays on the novel would do well to consult two fairly recent collections: Anna Snaith's *Palgrave Advances in Virginia Woolf Studies* (Palgrave, 2007) and Beth Rigel Daugherty and Mary Beth Pringle's *Approaches to Teaching Woolf's* To the Lighthouse (Modern Language Association of

America, 2001). Snaith's collection of essays is essential reading for students at all levels who want to conduct research on Virginia Woolf. Each chapter, written by a Woolf specialist, focuses on a different theoretical approach, from narratological to postmodernist and poststructuralist to European reception studies and much more. The MLA's *Approaches to Teaching* To the Lighthouse, although geared toward college and university professors, contains indispensible information about the novel and critical insights appropriate for secondary school teachers as well as college students. Serving as a reference book, it offers a detailed history of the novel's editions, provides an annotated bibliography of criticism arranged by theoretical approach, suggests further reading that will prepare students to get the most out of contemporary criticism, and includes lists of audiovisual and teaching materials relevant to the novel. The rest of the book provides smart, relatively brief readings of *To the Lighthouse* by respected scholar-teachers and editors of Woolf's writings.

Readers would also benefit from consulting additional reception histories of *To the Lighthouse*, such as Jane Goldman's *Virginia Woolf:* To the Lighthouse, The Waves (Icon Books, 1997; Columbia University Press, 1998), Suzanne Raitt's *Virginia Woolf's* To the Lighthouse (Palgrave Macmillan, 1990), Su Reid's *To the Lighthouse* (Palgrave Macmillan, 1991), and *The Reception of Virginia Woolf in Europe* edited by Mary Ann Caws and Nicola Luckhurst (Continuum, 2002).

EDITIONS OF *TO THE LIGHTHOUSE*

Throughout this book, I cite page references to the 1981 Harcourt edition of *To the Lighthouse*. The publishing history of *To the Lighthouse* is complex: Virginia Woolf approved "two different sets of proofs that then became two different first editions published on the same day, 5 May 1927" in Britain and the United States (Daugherty and Pringle 5; see, also, Dick, "Restless" 328 n5; Briggs, "Editing" 67; Silver, "Textual" 196). Consequently, US readers of the novel know *To the Lighthouse* from reading a copy of the first American edition (published by Houghton Mifflin Harcourt) while most UK readers are familiar with the first English edition (currently available from Penguin, Oxford University Press, Wordsworth, and Vintage) (Daugherty and Pringle 3–5). Which edition is in common use elsewhere varies by country. Complicating matters further, a third version, the Shakespeare Head Press edition (Blackwell, 1992) also circulates although at the time of this writing it is out of print. Edited by the Canadian Woolf scholar Susan Dick, this third representation of *To the Lighthouse* aims to present the authoritative version by using as the basis for the text page proofs for the first American edition corrected by Woolf's hand, which were not consistently incorporated into the 1927 publication (Daugherty and Pringle 4–5; see, also, Briggs, "Editing" 68–69; Dick, Introduction. *To the Lighthouse*. Shakespeare Head Press ed. xxxiii).

Readers would be well served by using either the Penguin Classics edition (Pearson, 2000) edited by Stella McNichol or the annotated Harvest Books edition (Harcourt, 2005) edited by Mark Hussey, which offer the most comprehensive scholarly information along with a text of the novel (UK and US versions, respectively). McNichol's edition, although based on the first English edition of *To the Lighthouse*, makes some changes to the narrative using the best available scholarly evidence. Along with footnotes and an introduction by Woolf biographer Hermione Lee, this edition includes a list of these changes as well as differences between the first English and American editions in its appendices (Daugherty and Pringle 4). Hussey's annotated edition, based on the first US edition, includes unobtrusive notes tucked discretely at the end of the book. Annotated and introduced by one of the foremost experts on Virginia Woolf, this edition also includes a detailed chronology of events in Woolf's life and suggestions for further reading. Ultimately, as Julia Briggs warns, one should keep in mind Woolf's "commitment to textual indeterminacy and to plentitude of meaning evident in the characteristic contrasts and dialectic generated by her work" ("Editing" 76).

Readers interested in studying the revisions Woolf made to *To the Lighthouse* should consult To the Lighthouse: *The Original Holograph Draft* edited by Susan Dick, a published transcription of Woolf's handwritten draft of the novel (University of Toronto Press, 1982). The manuscript is also available on microfilm as part of *The Virginia Woolf Manuscripts: From the Henry W. and Albert A. Berg Collection at the New York Public Library* (reel 7, Research Publications International, 1993).

In May 2002, the American edition of *To the Lighthouse* became available for purchase from Rosetta Books as an electronic book readable on a wireless mobile device. Several other publishers, such as MobileReference owned by SoundTells LLC, have subsequently followed suit. Most recently, on 24 February 2009, Amazon released its Kindle 2.0 to the US market, an updated version of its handheld mobile reading device. Using this device with an updated electronic edition of *To the Lighthouse* (Oak Grove, October 2008), readers can move between sections of the novel, search the novel for each occurrence of individual words, add annotations to the text, bookmark passages, and switch to the "text-to-speech" function, which allows a computer-synthesized voice (the reader controls "gender" and speed) to read the book aloud as the pages "turn" in synchronization. Audiobooks of *To the Lighthouse* are available as well on compact discs in both abridged and unabridged editions, featuring English actor Juliet Stevenson (Naxos AudioBooks, May 2008) and Scottish actor Phyllida Law (BBC Audiobooks, May 2004) as readers.

VIRTUAL WOOLF

Woolf's life in the virtual world of the Internet offers readers a wealth of information—from bibliographies to archival materials to Bloomsbury visual art to blogging to Second Life. The websites of the International Virginia Woolf Society and the Virginia Woolf Society of Great Britain should be readers' first stops when browsing the Web for Woolf-related information. They offer news about upcoming events for scholars and "common readers," access to online and published information about Woolf, and links to numerous other Woolf- and Bloomsbury-related websites. The International Virginia Woolf Society, which is based in North America, is primarily made up of professional academics from around the world—those not-so-common readers Woolf scorned (Cuddy-Keane 69). The Society sponsors an annual scholarly conference as well as Woolf-focused panels at other conventions and an online discussion group, Virginia Woolf (VW) Listserv. Although the listerv advertizes itself as being "open to all readers (scholarly and common) of Virginia Woolf" (see http://www.utoronto.ca/IVWS/), undergraduate students would be best served by first consulting some of the print and online sources listed here before venturing into the academic fray. The Society's bibliography of primary and secondary sources in Woolf studies is published yearly and, though not exhaustive, is essential for keeping up to date on books and articles pertaining to Woolf. (Go to http://www.utoronto.ca/IVWS/.)

The Virginia Woolf Society of Great Britain, which is composed of scholars and lay enthusiasts committed to promoting Woolf's reputation as a great writer, sponsors lectures, a reading group, and other events, primarily centered in London. The "useful links" page of the Society's website provides quick access to other Woolf- and Bloomsbury-related sites, including visual art collections of works by Vanessa Bell, Duncan Grant, and Roger Fry, national historic sites and other tourist spots connected to Woolf's life and art, and libraries and archives holding manuscripts and other Bloomsbury materials. The Society's journal, *The Virginia Woolf Bulletin*, which publishes previously unpublished Woolf letters as well as articles about her writing, lists the table of contents of each issue although it does not display the actual contents online. (Go to http://www.virginiawoolfsociety.co.uk/vw_links.htm.)

The Virginia Woolf Web, especially its "E-Text Guide and Collection Information" (http://orlando.jp.org/VWWARC/etext.html), is another useful site for those wanting quick access to full texts readable online. For example, this page provides links to several of the poems and the Grimms' fairy tale referenced in *To the Lighthouse* although as of this writing, several links are no longer functioning.

Woolf Online: An Electronic Edition and Commentary on Virginia Woolf's "Time Passes" has the potential to revolutionize the study of "Time Passes." The site allows one to view manuscripts from The Henry W. and Albert A. Berg Collection of English and American Literature, The New York City Public Library, alongside personal photographs from Woolf's family albums, relevant diary entries, book reviews, and other work Woolf composed at the time she was writing "Time Passes." The site offers viewers access to various digitalized versions of "Time Passes": Woolf's initial handwritten (holograph) draft; the 1926 typescript pages sent to Charles Mauron for translation; the printed proofs of the first Hogarth Press (UK) edition with Woolf's handwritten corrections, which she made for the Harcourt Brace (US) edition; and the text of four different published editions—the first UK edition, the first US edition, the Uniform edition, which Leonard and Virginia Woolf published in London in 1932, and the Everyman edition (part of the Everyman's Library Series) published in London in 1938. Accompanied by scholarly commentary, these materials documenting the history of Woolf's composition of *To the Lighthouse*'s most experimental section are arranged to facilitate close study and comparison. Created by Julia Briggs, Peter Shillingsburg, and Marilyn Deegan, with contributions from Mark Hussey, Nick Hayward, Marion Dell, Michael Lackey, and Alison Light,

> [t]he project aims to bring together the different stages of writing that went into the making of "Time Passes" to create a record of its development in the form of a genetic edition of the text, and to embed that edition in a network of histories and contexts that reconfigure traditional annotation techniques as a system of linked but separate strands of thought, thus producing a new form of literary archaeology.

For more information and to enter the site, go to www.woolfonline. com.

For readers wanting informative, interactive sites tailored to Woolf's "common readers," *Blogging Woolf: Focusing on Virginia Woolf and Her Circle, Past and Present,* created, written, and edited by Paula Maggio, and *Second Life: Woolf World* created by Elisa Kay Sparks and her students at Clemson University, are also available. *Blogging Woolf* features announcements on upcoming events and recent publications pertaining to Woolf, Bloomsbury travel destinations, consumer goods bearing Woolf's likeness, and online commentary. One section of the blog, "Woolf Sightings," lists contemporary references to Woolf in the print and broadcast media, music, and other forms of popular culture. (Go to http://blogging-woolf.wordpress.com/.) *Second Life: Woolf World* allows the user to enter into and interact through an avatar in a virtual world comprised of rooms and artifacts from Woolf's life. (Go to http://21woolfworld.blogspot.com/.)

Alternatively, for readers interested in Woolf's influence on today's writers, the English novelist Jeanette Winterson's website is worth a visit. Although devoted to promoting Winterson's writing, its forum hosts online reading groups in modern literature—subscribers discussed *To the Lighthouse* in November 2008. A self-declared literary descendent of Woolf, Winterson, in her book *Art Objects: Essays on Ecstasy and Effrontery* (Vintage, 1997), writes about *Orlando* and *The Waves* in her essays "A Gift of Wings" and "A Veil of Words." Winterson is the commissioning editor for the

Vintage Classics editions of Woolf's novels. On her website, she explains her reasons for commissioning contemporary writers for the novels' introductions in addition to critics. Irish poet Eavan Boland and modernist scholar Maud Ellmann introduce *To the Lighthouse*. (Go to http://www.jeanettewinterson.com/pages/content/index.asp?PageID=249.)

REFERENCE WORKS, BIBLIOGRAPHIES, AND OTHER RESOURCES FOR RESEARCH

Mark Hussey's *Virginia Woolf A to Z: The Essential Reference to Her Life and Writings* (Oxford University Press, 1995) is a vital source of information for "common readers" and determined researchers alike. An encyclopedia of information about Woolf's life and writings, it contains detailed plot descriptions, accounts of creative inception, reception histories, and summaries of contemporary criticism, all arranged alphabetically for quick consultation. Other indispensible reference works include *Virginia Woolf: The Critical Heritage* edited by Robin Majumdar and Allen McLaurin (Routledge, 1997) and *A Bibliography of Virginia Woolf* edited by B. J. Kirkpatrick and Stuart Clarke (4th edition, Oxford University Press, 1998). Majumdar and McLaurin's book contains difficult to obtain early reviews of Woolf's works arranged by their titles. Kirkpatrick and Clarke's book is a comprehensive annotated bibliography of primary and secondary texts, including Woolf's letters to newspapers (signed and unsigned), uncollected letters published in books and articles, and locations for Woolf's existing manuscripts housed in collections. Additionally, the scholarly journal *Modern Fiction Studies* has published extensive selected bibliographies of Woolf criticism beginning in 1956 (by Maurice Beebe), and supplemented by publications in 1972 (by Barbara Weiser), 1992 (by Laura Sue Fuderer), and 2004 (by Justine Dymond).

For full-text critical articles, students should consult the published proceedings of the International Virginia Woolf Society's annual conferences (Pace University Press, nos. 1–10, conference years 1991–2000; Clemson University Digital Press, nos. 13, 15–17, conference years 2004, 2006–2008; online viewing for a fee at the Center for Virginia Woolf Studies [http://www.csub.edu/woolf_center/], nos. 12–16, conference years 2002–2006). Scholarly journals devoted to Virginia Woolf studies include *Woolf Studies Annual* (Pace University Press, 1995 to the present) as well as the following special issues: *Journal of the Short Story in English* 50 (spring 2008, available online), *Modern Fiction Studies* (see special Woolf issues in 1956 [vol. 2, no. 1], 1972 [vol. 18, no. 3], 1992 [vol. 38, no. 1], and 2004 [vol. 50, no. 1]), *The South Carolina Review* (see special Woolf issue in fall 1996 [vol. 29, no. 1], available online), *Twentieth Century Literature* (vol. 25, 1979), and *Women's Studies* (vol. 4, 1977).

BIOGRAPHIES AND BLOOMSBURY

For detailed information about Virginia Woolf's life, Hermione Lee's *Virginia Woolf* (Vintage, 1999) and Julia Briggs's *Virginia Woolf: An Inner Life* (Allen Lane, 2005) are engagingly written, scholarly biographies. Briggs's is organized by Woolf's major works with chapter 7 "Writing Itself" devoted to *To the Lighthouse*. Lee arranges her subject by topic, such as "Abuses," "Subversives," and "Fascism." Alison Light's *Mrs. Woolf and the Servants: An Intimate History of Domestic Life in Bloomsbury* (Bloomsbury Press, 2008) provides the most comprehensive information to date about Virginia Woolf's relationships with her servants in the context of their own lives and the history of domestic work in Britain in the late nineteenth and early twentieth centuries.

For readers wanting to learn more about the Bloomsbury Group, S. P. Rosenbaum's books are an excellent place to start. *The Bloomsbury Group: A Collection of Memoirs, Commentary and Criticism* makes available in one volume excerpts from a wide range of sources by and about Bloomsbury, which Rosenbaum contextualizes with informative introductory comments (Croom Helm, 1975). *A Bloomsbury Group Reader* (Blackwell, 1993) includes complete versions of short essays written by such Bloomsbury members as Virginia Woolf, E. M. Forster, Lytton Strachey, and John Maynard Keynes, giving a cross-section of their concerns, from Post-Impressionism and psychoanalysis to censorship and women's rights. For scholarly accounts of Bloomsbury, see Rosenbaum's *Aspects of Bloomsbury: Studies in Modern English Literary and Intellectual History* (St. Martin's, 1998) and his three-volume *Victorian Bloomsbury: The Early Literary History of the Bloomsbury Group* (St. Martin's, 1987), *Edwardian Bloomsbury: The Early Literary History of the Bloomsbury Group* (Palgrave Macmillan, 1994), and *Georgian Bloomsbury: The Early Literary History of the Bloomsbury Group* (Palgrave Macmillan, 2004).

WOOLF AND POSTSTRUCTURALISM

Several of the essays discussed in chapter 4 exemplify poststructural- ist readings of *To the Lighthouse* in that their arguments are based on certain assumptions about language, representation, meaning, and identity. Specifically, they assume that language functions as a closed system of "signs," the meanings of which are determined through their differences from each other rather than by any inherent link to absolute values; language and linguistic representation are not neu- tral nor do they passively reflect existing realities, but rather they reproduce hierarchies structured within language itself; and gender, race, and sexuality are socially constructed categories of identity rather than biologically determined truths, yet their social meanings produce material effects. Readers interested in learning more about the impact of poststructuralist theory on Woolf studies should begin by reading Pamela Caughie's "Postmodernist and Poststruc- turalist Approaches," chapter 7 of Anna Snaith's *Palgrave Advances in Virginia Woolf Studies*. For poststructuralist critical analyses of *To the Lighthouse*, see, in particular, David Sherman's "A Plot Unraveling into Ethics: Woolf, Levinas, and 'Time Passes'" (2007), Emily Dalgarno's *Virginia Woolf and the Visible World* (Cambridge University Press, 2001) (see 22–27, 84–96, 140–42), Caughie's "Returning to the Lighthouse: A Postmodern Approach" in Beth Rigel Daugherty and Mary Beth Pringle's *Approaches to Teaching* To the Lighthouse, and Caughie's *Virginia Woolf and Postmodernism: Literature in Quest and Question of Itself* (Illinois University Press, 1991) (see 33–39).

CRITICAL ESSAYS ON *TO THE LIGHTHOUSE*, PHILOSOPHY, AND PHYSICS

Numerous essays have been written about the philosophers influ- encing Woolf as she shaped *To the Lighthouse*'s discussion of Mr. Ramsay and developed the ideas underpinning her novel and its experimental prose. Critics have also compared early-twentieth- century breakthroughs in theoretical physics to Woolf's treatment of time and space in *To the Lighthouse*. In addition to Ann Banfield's book *The Phantom Table: Woolf, Fry, Russell and the Epistemology of Modernism* (Cambridge University Press, 2000) and her essay "Time Passes: Virginia Woolf, Post-Impressionism, and Cambridge

Time" (2003), readers should consult the following essays: Michael Lackey's "Modernist Anti-Philosophicalism and Virginia Woolf's Critique of Philosophy" (2006); Eric Hayot's "Bertrand Russell's Chinese Eyes: Modern Chinese Literature and Culture" (2006) (more about searching for the origins of modernism than about *To the Lighthouse*); Sharon Stockton's "Public Space and Private Time: Perspective in *To the Lighthouse* and in Einstein's Special Theory" (1998); Mark Hussey's "*To the Lighthouse* and Physics: The Cosmology of David Bohm and Virginia Woolf" (1995); Sandra Donaldson's "Where Does Q Leave Mr. Ramsay?" (1992); Deborah Esch's "'Think of a Kitchen Table': Hume, Woolf, and the Translation of Example" (1987); and Gillian Beer's "Hume, Stephen, and Elegy in *To the Lighthouse*" (1984).

VIRGINIA WOOLF'S OTHER WRITINGS

Novels

The Voyage Out (1915)
Night and Day (1919)
Jacob's Room (1922)
Mrs. Dalloway (1925)
Orlando: A Biography (1928)
The Waves (1931)
The Years (1937)
Between the Acts (1941)

Earlier Versions of Novels

The Pargiters: The Novel-Essay Portion of The Years (Ed. Mitchell Leaska, 1977)
Melymbrosia: An Early Version of The Voyage Out (Ed. Louise DeSalvo, 1982)

Short Stories

The Mark on the Wall (1917)
Kew Gardens (1919)
Monday or Tuesday (1921)
A Haunted House and Other Short Stories (1944)
Nurse Lugton's Golden Thimble (1966)
Mrs. Dalloway's Party: A Short Story Sequence (Ed. Stella McNichol, 1973)
The Complete Shorter Fiction (Ed. Susan Dick, 2nd ed., 1989)

Drama

Freshwater: A Comedy (Ed. Lucio Ruotolo, 1976)

Essays

Mr. Bennett and Mrs. Brown (1924)
The Common Reader (1925)
A Room of One's Own (1929)
The Second Common Reader (1932)
Three Guineas (1938)
The Death of the Moth and Other Essays (Ed. Leonard Woolf, 1942)
The Moment and Other Essays (Ed. Leonard Woolf, 1947)
The Captain's Death Bed and Other Essays (Ed. Leonard Woolf, 1950)
Granite and Rainbow: Essays (Ed. Leonard Woolf, 1958)
On Being Ill (2002)
Carlyle's House and Other Sketches (Ed. David Bradshaw, 2003)
The London Scene: Six Essays on London Life (2006)
The Essays of Virginia Woolf (Ed. Andrew McNeillie, 1986–1994 [vols. 1–4];
    Ed. Stuart Clarke, 2009 [vol. 5]; 5 vols. to date)

Letters

The Letters of Virginia Woolf (Ed. Nigel Nicolson and Joanne Trautmann,
    1975–1980; 6 vols.)
Congenial Spirits: The Selected Letters of Virginia Woolf (Ed. Joanne Traut-
    mann Banks, 1989)

Diaries

The Diary of Virginia Woolf (Ed. Anne Olivier Bell, 1977–79; 5 vols.)
A Passionate Apprentice: The Early Journals 1897–1909 (Ed. Mitchell Leaska,
    1990)

Biography and Memoir

Flush: A Biography (1933)
Roger Fry: A Biography (1940)
Moments of Being (Ed. Jeanne Schulkind, 2nd ed., 1985)

Juvenilia

A Cockney's Farming Experiences (Ed. Suzanne Henig, 1972)
Hyde Park Gate News: The Stephen Family Newspaper (By Virginia Woolf
    and Vanessa Bell with Thoby Stephen; Ed. Gill Lowe, 2005)

WORKS CITED

Abel, Elizabeth. "Matrilineage and the Racial 'Other': Woolf and Her Literary Daughters of the Second Wave." Featured Presentation. 3rd Annual Conference on Virginia Woolf. Lincoln University, Lincoln, Nebraska. 13 June 1993.

—. *Virginia Woolf and the Fictions of Psychoanalysis*. Chicago: U of Chicago P, 1989.

Aiken, Conrad. "The Novel as Work of Art." *The Dial* 83 (July 1927): 41–44. Rpt. in Beja, *Critical* 15–17.

Albee, Edward. *Who's Afraid of Virginia Woolf?* New York: Penguin, 1962.

Andrews, Marilyn. *To the Lighthouse: Lily Briscoe's Painting*. 2008. Mixed media. Private collection. Web. 27 Nov. 2008. http://www.marilynandrewssculpture.com/2008/pages/10.

—. *To the Lighthouse: Mrs. Ramsay's Knitting*. 2008. Mixed media. Private collection. Web. 27 Nov. 2008. http://www.marilynandrewssculpture.com/2008/pages/14.html.

Annan, Noel. "Bloomsbury and the Leavises." Marcus, *Virginia Woolf and Bloomsbury* 23–38.

Anscombe, Isabelle. *Omega and After: Bloomsbury and the Decorative Arts*. London: Thames and Hudson, 1981.

Anson, George. *A Voyage Round the World: In the Years 1740, 1741, 1742, 1743, 1744*. Comp. Richard Walter. 1748. London: Printed for the Society for Promoting Christian Knowledge, 1845.

Atkin, Jonathan. *A War of Individuals: Bloomsbury Attitudes to the Great War*. Manchester: Manchester UP, 2002.

Auerbach, Erich. *Mimesis: The Representation of Reality in Western Literature*. Trans. Willard Trask. Garden City: Doubleday Anchor Books, 1957.

Baldanza, Frank. "*To the Lighthouse* Again." *PMLA* 70.3 (June 1955): 548–52.

Banfield, Ann. *The Phantom Table: Woolf, Fry, Russell and the Epistemology of Modernism*. Cambridge: Cambridge UP, 2000.

—. "Time Passes: Virginia Woolf, Post-Impressionism, and Cambridge Time." *Poetics Today* 24.3 (Fall 2003): 471–516.

Barrett, Eileen and Patricia Cramer, eds. *Re: Reading, Re: Writing, Re: Teaching Virginia Woolf: Selected Papers from the Fourth Annual Conference on Virginia Woolf*. New York: Pace UP, 1995.

—, eds. *Virginia Woolf: Lesbian Readings*. New York: New York UP, 1997.

Barthes, Roland. "The Death of the Author." *Image Music Text*. Trans. Stephen Heath. New York: Hill and Wang, 1977. 142–48.

—. "From Work to Text." *Image Music Text*. Trans. Stephen Heath. New York: Hill and Wang, 1977. 155–64.

—. *S/Z: An Essay*. Trans. Richard Miller. New York: Hill and Wang, 1974.

Beach, Joseph Warren. "Virginia Woolf." *The English Journal* 26.8 (Oct. 1937): 603–12.

Beebe, Maurice. "Criticism of Virginia Woolf: A Selected Checklist with an Index to Studies of Separate Works." *Modern Fiction Studies* 2.1 (1956): 36-45.

Beer, Gillian. "Hume, Stephen, and Elegy in *To the Lighthouse*." *Essays in Criticism: A Quarterly Journal of Literary Criticism* 34.1 (Jan. 1984): 33–55.

Beja, Morris, ed. *Critical Essays on Virginia Woolf*. Boston: G. K. Hall, 1985.

—. *Virginia Woolf:* To the Lighthouse, *A Casebook*. London: Macmillan, 1970.

Bell, Clive. *Old Friends: Personal Recollections*. London: Chatto & Windus, 1956.

Bell, Lindsay. "Transmitting the Voices, Voyages and Visions: Adapting Virginia Woolf's *To the Lighthouse* for Radio." *Languages of Theatre Shaped by Women*. Ed. Jane de Gay and Lizbeth Goodman. Bristol: Intellect, 2001. 73–88.

Bell, Quentin. "Vanessa Bell and Duncan Grant." *Crafts* 42 (Jan./Feb. 1980): 26–33.

—. *Virginia Woolf: A Biography*. 2 vols. New York: Harcourt, 1972.

Bell, Vanessa. Dust jacket design for *To the Lighthouse*. 1927. V. Woolf, To the Lighthouse: *The Original Holograph Draft* 41. Print.

—. Lighthouse fireplace surround. 1930. Gillespie, *Sisters'* 158. Plate 3.23. Print.

—. "Notes on Bloomsbury." 1951. Rosenbaum, *Collection* 73–84.

—. "Notes on Virginia's Childhood." 1974. Rosenbaum, *Reader* 331–35.

—. *The Nursery*. 1930–32. Location unknown. Gillespie, *Sisters'* 160. Plate 3.24. Print.

—. *Selected Letters of Vanessa Bell*. Ed. Regina Marler. New York: Pantheon, 1993.

Bellamy, Suzanne. "Artist's Statement." Web. 27 Nov. 2008. http://home. goulburn.net.au/~sbellamy/.

—. "'Painting the Words': A Version of Lily Briscoe's Paintings from *To the Lighthouse*." *Virginia Woolf Turning the Centuries: Selected Papers from the Ninth Annual Conference on Virginia Woolf*. Ed. Ann Ardis and Bonnie Kime Scott. New York: Pace UP, 2000. 244–51.

—. "The Pattern behind the Words." Barrett and Cramer, *Virginia Woolf: Lesbian* 21–36.

—. *Seeing Through a Film of Yellow*. 2002. Painting. Private collection. Web. 27 Nov. 2008. http://home.goulburn.net.au/~sbellamy/.

—. *To the Lighthouse* (triptych). 1999. Painting. Private collection. Web. 27 Nov. 2008. http://home.goulburn.net.au/~sbellamy/.

—. *Water*. 2003. Painting. Private collection. Web. 27 Nov. 2008. http://home. goulburn.net.au/~sbellamy/.

—. *The Waves*. 2000. Painting. Private collection. Web. 27 Nov. 2008. http:// home.goulburn.net.au/~sbellamy/.

—. *Woolf's London*. 2002. Painting. Private collection. Web. 27 Nov. 2008. http://home.goulburn.net.au/~sbellamy/.

—. *Woolfworld*. 2002. Mixed media. Private collection. Web. 27 Nov. 2008. http://home.goulburn.net.au/~sbellamy/.

Bennett, Arnold. Rev. of *To the Lighthouse*, by Virginia Woolf. *Evening Standard* 23 June 1927: 5. Majumdar and McLaurin 200–01.

Bennett, Joan. *Virginia Woolf: Her Art as a Novelist.* 1945. Cambridge: Cambridge UP, 1964.

Bennett, Paula. "The Mother's Part: Incest and Maternal Deprivation in Woolf and Morrison." *Narrating Mothers: Theorizing Maternal Subjectivites.* Ed. Brenda Daly and Maureen Reddy. Knoxville: U of Tennessee P, 1991. 125–38.

Bergson, Henri. *Time and Free Will: An Essay on the Immediate Data of Consciousness.* 1910. Trans. F. L. Pogson. London: George Allen & Unwin Ltd., 1950.

Billington, Michael. "Theatre: To the Lighthouse, Lyric Studio." *Guardian* 7 Jan. 1995: 28.

Black, Jeremy and Donald MacRaid. *Nineteenth-Century Britain.* New York: Palgrave Macmillan, 2002.

Black, Naomi. "Virginia Woolf and the Women's Movement." *Virginia Woolf: A Feminist Slant.* Ed. Jane Marcus. Lincoln: U of Nebraska P, 1983. 180–97.

Blogging Woolf: Focusing on Virginia Woolf and Her Circle, Past and Present. Created, written, and ed. Paula Maggio. N.p. Web. 3 March 2009. http://bloggingwoolf.wordpress.com/.

Blotner, Joseph. "Mythic Patterns in *To the Lighthouse.*" *PMLA* 71.4 (Sept. 1956): 547–62.

Briggs, Julia. "Editing Virginia Woolf for the Nineties." *The South Carolina Review* 29.1 (Fall 1996): 67–77.

—. *Virginia Woolf: An Inner Life.* London: Allen Lane, 2005.

Brogan, Howard. "Science and Narrative Structure in Austen, Hardy, and Woolf." *Nineteenth-Century Fiction* 11.4 (March 1957): 276–87.

Browne, William. "The Sirens' Song." 1614. *Virginia Woolf Web.* Archive, 1995–99. Web. 15 Nov. 2008. http://orlando.jp.org/VWWARC/DAT/browne.html.

Bullock, Ken. "The Theater: Berkeley Rep's 'Lighthouse.'" *Berkeley Daily Planet* 6 March 2007. Web. 23 Nov. 2008.

Cardus, Neville. "The Hallé Concert." *Manchester Guardian* 5 Feb. 1932, city ed.: 11.

Caughie, Pamela. "How Do We Keep Desire from Passing with Beauty?" *Tulsa Studies in Women's Literature* 19.2 (2000): 269–84.

—. "Postmodernist and Poststructuralist Approaches." Snaith 143–68.

—. "Returning to the Lighthouse: A Postmodern Approach." Daugherty and Pringle 47–53.

—. *Virginia Woolf and Postmodernism: Literature in Quest and Question of Itself.* Urbana: U of Illinois P, 1991.

Caws, Mary Ann and Nicola Luckhurst, eds. *The Reception of Virginia Woolf in Europe.* London: Continuum Books, 2002.

Chantler, Ashley. "The Castaway." *The Literary Encyclopedia.* Ed. Robert Clark, Emory Elliott, and Janet Todd. The Literary Dictionary Company Ltd. 18 Jan. 2007. Web. 1 Aug. 2008. http://www.litencyc.com/.

Chicago, Judy. *The Dinner Party.* 1974–79. Mixed media. Elizabeth Sackler Center for Feminist Art. Brooklyn Museum, New York. Web. 23 Nov. 2008.

http://www.brooklynmuseum.org/eascfa/dinner_party/place_settings/virginia_woolf.php.

Childers, Joseph and Gary Hentzi, eds. *The Columbia Dictionary of Modern Literary and Cultural Criticism.* New York: Columbia UP, 1995.

Clewell, Tammy. "Consolation Refused: Virginia Woolf, the Great War, and Modernist Mourning." *Modern Fiction Studies* 50.1 (Spring 2004): 197–223.

Cliff, Michelle. "Virginia Woolf and the Imperial Gaze: A Glance Askance." *Virginia Woolf Emerging Perspectives: Selected Papers from the Third Annual Conference on Virginia Woolf.* Ed. Mark Hussey and Vara Neverow. New York: Pace UP, 1994. 91–102.

Connema, Richard. "A Complicated Production of Virginia Woolf's *To the Lighthouse.*" *Talkin' Broadway* Feb. 2007. Web. 23 Nov. 2008.

Cook, Blanche Wiesen. "'Women Alone Stir My Imagination': Lesbianism and the Cultural Tradition." *Signs* 4.4 (Summer 1979): 718–39.

"Co-operative Women's Guild." National Co-operative Archive. Co-operative College. Manchester, UK. Web. 20 July 2008. http://archive.co-op.ac.uk/cwg.htm.

"Co-operative Women's Guild." Women's Studies Subject Guide. University Archives. University of Hull. Hull, UK. Web. 20 July 2008. http://www.hull.ac.uk/arc/collection/womensstudies/cwg.html.

Cowper, William. "The Castaway." 1803. *Virginia Woolf Web.* Archive, 1995–99. Web. 15 Nov. 2008. http://orlando.jp.org/VWWARC/DAT/castaway.html.

Craig, Pat. "'Lighthouse' Illuminating Play—Berkeley Rep Shows Woolf's Prose In a Fresh and Innovative New Light." *Contra Costa Times* 1 March 2007, final ed.: D3.

Cuddy-Keane, Melba. *Virginia Woolf, the Intellectual, and the Public Sphere.* Cambridge: Cambridge UP, 2003.

Cunningham, Michael. *The Hours.* New York: Farrar, Straus and Giroux, 1998.

Daiches, David. *Virginia Woolf.* Norfolk: New Directions Books, 1942.

Dalgarno, Emily. *Virginia Woolf and the Visible World.* Cambridge: Cambridge UP, 2001.

Daugherty, Beth Rigel. "Readin', Writin', and Revisin': Virginia Woolf's 'How Should One Read a Book?'" Rosenberg and Dubino 155–79.

—. "Virginia Woolf's 'How Should One Read a Book?'" *Woolf Studies Annual* 4 (May 1998): 123–85.

Daugherty, Beth Rigel and Mary Beth Pringle. *Approaches to Teaching Woolf's* To the Lighthouse. New York: Modern Language Association of America, 2001.

de Gay, Jane. "Behind the Purple Triangle: Art and Iconography in *To the Lighthouse.*" *Woolf Studies Annual* 5 (1999): 1–23.

Dell, Marion. *Peering Through the Escallonia: Virginia Woolf, Talland House and St Ives.* Bloomsbury Heritage Series. London: Cecil Woolf, 1999.

Derbyshire, S. H. "An Analysis of Mrs. Woolf's *To the Lighthouse.*" *College English* 3.4 (Jan. 1942): 353–60.

DeSalvo, Louise. "Lighting the Cave: The Relationship between Vita Sackville-West and Virginia Woolf." *Signs* 8.2 (Winter 1982): 195–214.

—. *Virginia Woolf: The Impact of Childhood Sexual Abuse on Her Life and Work*. New York: Ballantine Books, 1989.

Dick, Susan. Introduction. *To the Lighthouse*. By Virginia Woolf. Shakespeare Head Press edition. Oxford: Blackwell, 1992. xi–xxxvii.

—. Introduction. To the Lighthouse: *The Original Holograph Draft*. Ed. Susan Dick. Toronto: U of Toronto P, 1982. 11–35.

—. "The Restless Searcher: A Discussion of the Evolution of 'Time Passes' in *To the Lighthouse*." *English Studies in Canada* 3 (Autumn 1979): 311–29.

—, ed. *To the Lighthouse*. By Virginia Woolf. Shakespeare Head Press edition. Oxford: Blackwell, 1992.

Dolan, Jill. *The Feminist Spectator as Critic*. Ann Arbor: U of Michigan P, 1991.

Donaldson, Sandra. "Where Does Q Leave Mr. Ramsay?" *Tulsa Studies in Women's Literature* 11.2 (Autumn 1992): 329–36.

Doyle, Laura. "'These Emotions of the Body': Intercorporeal Narrative in *To the Lighthouse*." *Twentieth Century Literature* 40 (1994): 42–71.

—. "Transnational History at Our Backs: A Long View of Larsen, Woolf, and Queer Racial Subjectivity in Atlantic Modernism." *Modernism/modernity* 13.3 (2006): 531–59.

—. "Voyaging Beyond the Race Mother: *Melymbrosia* and *To the Lighthouse*." *Bordering on the Body: The Racial Matrix of Modern Fiction and Culture*. By Doyle. Oxford: Oxford UP, 1994. 139–73.

D'Souza, Karen. "The Zen Director: Les Waters Unearths Complex Themes in Berkeley Rep's 'Lighthouse.'" *San Jose Mercury News* 4 March 2007: 5D, 8D.

Dymond, Justine. "Virginia Woolf Scholarship from 1991 to 2003: A Selected Bibliography." *Modern Fiction Studies* 50.1 (Spring 2004): 241–79.

Eliot, T. S. "Virginia Woolf." Rosenbaum, *Collection* 202–03. Rpt. of "Virginia Woolf." *Horizon* 3 (May 1941): 314–16.

—. *The Waste Land*. London: Hogarth Press, 1922.

Elton, Charles. "A Garden Song" ["Luriana, Lurilee"]. 1945. *Virginia Woolf Web*. Archive, 1995–99. Web. 15 Nov. 2008. http://orlando.jp.org/VWWARC/DAT/luriana.html.

Emery, Mary Lou. "'Robbed of Meaning': The Work at the Center of *To the Lighthouse*." *Modern Fiction Studies* 38.1 (Spring 1992): 217–34.

Empson, William. "Virginia Woolf." *Scrutinies*. Vol. 2. Ed. Edgell Rickword. London: Wishart, 1931. 203–16.

Epes, Isota Tucker. *Two Ways of Seeing*. Painting. N.d. Private collection. Web. 27 Nov. 2008. http://www.ecva.org/exhibition/VPPreview/artists3/epes2.html.

Esch, Deborah. "'Think of a Kitchen Table': Hume, Woolf, and the Translation of Example." *Literature as Philosophy/Philosophy as Literature*. Ed. Donald Marshall. Iowa City: U of Iowa P, 1987. 262–76.

Faulkner, William. *The Sound and the Fury*. 1929. New York: Vintage, 1991.

"Femina Vie Heureuse Prize: English Committee: Minutes and Papers." *National Archives*. UK Archives Network. Web. 7 Nov. 2008. http://www.nationalarchives.gov.uk.

Flint, Kate. "Virginia Woolf and the General Strike." *Essays in Criticism: A Quarterly Journal of Literary Criticism* 36.4 (Oct. 1986): 319–34.

Forster, E. M. *A Passage to India*. 1924. New York: Harvest, 1965.

—. "Virginia Woolf." 1942. *Two Cheers for Democracy*. By Forster. New York: Harcourt, 1951.

Friedman, Norman. "The Waters of Annihilation: Double Vision in *To the Lighthouse*." *ELH* 22.1 (March 1955): 61–79.

Friedman, Susan Stanford. *Mappings: Feminism and the Cultural Geographies of Encounter*. Princeton: Princeton UP, 1998.

Froula, Christine. *Virginia Woolf and the Bloomsbury Avant-Garde: War, Civilization, Modernity*. New York: Columbia UP, 2005.

Fry, Roger. "An Essay in Aesthetics." 1909. *Vision and Design*. By Fry. London: Chatto & Windus, 1920. 11–25.

—. *Letters of Roger Fry*. Vol. 2. Ed. Denys Sutton. London: Chatto & Windus, 1972.

Fuderer, Laura Sue. "Criticism of Virginia Woolf from 1972 to December 1990: A Selected Checklist." *Modern Fiction Studies* 38.1 (Spring 1992): 303-42.

Funke, Lewis. "News of the Rialto: Burnett." *New York Times* 18 Nov. 1962: X1.

Gabler, Hans Walter. "A Tale of Two Texts: Or, How One Might Edit Virginia Woolf's *To the Lighthouse*." *Woolf Studies Annual* 10 (2004): 1–29.

Gerzina, Gretchen Holbrook. "Bushmen and Blackface: Bloomsbury and 'Race.'" *The South Carolina Review* 38.2 (Spring 2006): 46–64.

Gillespie, Diane Filby. "Dorothy Richardson." B. Scott 393–99.

—. "May Sinclair." B. Scott 436–42.

—. *The Sisters' Arts: The Writing and Painting of Virginia Woolf and Vanessa Bell*. Syracuse: Syracuse UP, 1988.

Goldman, Jane. *The Feminist Aesthetics of Virginia Woolf: Modernism, Post-Impressionism and the Politics of the Visual*. Cambridge: Cambridge UP, 1998.

—. "Modernist Studies." Snaith 35–59.

—, ed. *Virginia Woolf: To the Lighthouse, The Waves*. New York: Columbia UP, 1998.

Gonzalez, Ed. Rev. of *Evening. Slant Magazine* 19 June 2007. Web. 23 Nov. 2008.

Goring, Paul. "The Shape of *To the Lighthouse*: Lily Briscoe's Painting and the Reader's Vision." *Word & Image* 10.3 (July-Sept 1994): 222–29.

Grant, Duncan. "Virginia Woolf." Rosenbaum, *Collection* 65–68. Rpt. of "Virginia Woolf." *Horizon* 3 (June 1941): 402–06.

Grimm, Jacob and Wilhelm Grimm. "The Fisherman and His Wife." 1812. Trans. Margaret Hunt. "19th-Century German Stories: Fairy Tales by the Grimm Brothers." Website of Robert Godwin-Jones. School of World

Studies. Virginia Commonwealth University. Web. 31 July 2008. http://www.fln.vcu.edu/grimm/fischer_e.html.

Guth, Deborah. "Virginia Woolf: Myth and *To the Lighthouse.*" *College Literature* 11.3 (Fall 1984): 233–49.

Hafley, James. *The Glass Roof: Virginia Woolf as Novelist.* Berkeley: U of California P, 1954.

Hartgrave, Lee. "Sweepingly Beautiful 'To the Lighthouse.'" *Beyond Chron* 2 March 2007. Web. 23 Nov. 2008.

Hartley, Lodowick. 1939. "Of Time and Mrs. Woolf." Vogler 97–98.

Harvey, Dennis. *Variety* (digital edition) 1 March 2007. Web. 23 Nov. 2008.

Haule, James. "'Le Temps passe' and the Original Typescript: An Early Version of the 'Time Passes' Section of *To the Lighthouse.*" *Twentieth Century Literature* 29.3 (Fall 1983): 267–311.

—. *"To the Lighthouse* and the Great War: The Evidence of Virginia Woolf's Revisions of 'Time Passes.'" Hussey, *Virginia Woolf and War* 164–79.

Hayot, Eric. "Bertrand Russell's Chinese Eyes." *Modern Chinese Literature and Culture* 18.1 (2006): 120–54.

Heilbrun, Carolyn. *"To the Lighthouse*: The New Story of Mother and Daughter." *ADE Bulletin* 87 (Fall 1987): 12–14.

—. *Toward a Recognition of Androgyny.* New York: Knopf, 1973.

Henke, Suzette. "Virginia Woolf's *To the Lighthouse*: In Defense of the Woman Artist." *Virginia Woolf Quarterly* 2.1–2 (1975): 39–47.

Holroyd, Michael. "Bloomsbury and the Fabians." Marcus, *Virginia Woolf and Bloomsbury* 39–51.

Homer. *The Odyssey.* Trans. Samuel Butler. Project Gutenberg. 4 Jan. 1999. Etext-No. 1727. Web. 5 Aug. 2008. http://www.gutenberg.org/etext/1727.

The Hours. Screenplay by David Hare. Dir. Stephen Daldry. Perf. Nicole Kidman, Julianne Moore, and Meryl Streep. Paramount, 2002. Film.

Humm, Maggie. *Modernist Women and Visual Cultures: Virginia Woolf, Vanessa Bell, Photography and Cinema.* New Brunswick: Rutgers UP, 2003.

Hurka, Thomas. "Moore's Moral Philosophy." *The Stanford Encyclopedia of Philosophy.* Ed. Edward Zalta. Fall 2008 ed. Web. 1 Aug. 2008. http://plato.stanford.edu/archives/fall2008/entries/moore-moral/.

Hussey, Mark. Introduction. *To the Lighthouse.* By Virginia Woolf. Ed. Hussey. New York: Harcourt, 2005. xxxv–lxviii.

—, ed. *To the Lighthouse.* By Virginia Woolf. New York: Harcourt, 2005.

—. *"To the Lighthouse* and Physics: The Cosmology of David Bohm and Virginia Woolf." *New Essays on Virginia Woolf.* Ed. Helen Wussow. Dallas: Contemporary Research Press, 1995. 79–98.

—, ed. *Virginia Woolf and War: Fiction, Reality, and Myth.* Syracuse: Syracuse UP, 1991.

—. *Virginia Woolf A to Z: A Comprehensive Reference for Students, Teachers and Common Readers to Her Life, Work and Critical Reception.* Oxford: Oxford UP, 1995.

Hutcheon, Linda. *Formalism and the Freudian Aesthetic: The Example of Charles Mauron.* Cambridge: Cambridge UP, 2006.

Irvine, A. D. "Bertrand Russell." *The Stanford Encyclopedia of Philosophy.* Ed. Edward Zalta. Fall 2008 ed. Web. 10 March 2009. http://plato.stanford.edu/entries/russell/.

Isherwood, Charles. "To Woolf's 'Lighthouse,' Where Things Are Better Left Unsaid." *New York Times* 3 March 2007: B13.

it was this: it was this:. Chor. by Stephen Pelton in collaboration with Christy Funsch and Nol Simonse. Stephen Pelton Dance Theater. Perf. by Christy Funsch and Nol Simonse. Pope Auditorium, Fordham University, New York. 5 June 2009. Performance.

"'J'accuse . . . !' Émile Zola, L'Aurore and the Dreyfus Affair." "The Dreyfus Affair and Anti-Semitism." *Virtual Absinthe Museum.* Oxygénée, Ltd. N.d. Web. 6 June 2008. http://www.oxygenee.com/Zola-and-Dreyfus.pdf.

Jacobus, Mary. "'The Third Stroke': Reading Woolf with Freud." *Grafts: Feminist Cultural Criticism.* Ed. Susan Sheridan. London: Verso, 1988. 93–110.

Jones, Chad. Rev. *To the Lighthouse*, Berkeley Repertory Theatre. *Theater Dogs: Backstage with Chad Jones.* 1 March 2007. *InsideBayArea.com* (ANG Newspapers). Web. 23 Nov. 2008.

Joyce, James. *Dubliners.* 1914. Norton Critical Edition. New York: Norton, 2006.

—. *A Portrait of the Artist as a Young Man.* 1916. New York: Penguin, 2002.

—. *Ulysses.* 1922. Ed. Hans Walter Gabler. New York: Vintage, 1986.

Karras, Ruth Mazo. *From Boys to Men: Formations of Masculinity in Late Medieval Europe.* Philadelphia: U of Pennsylvania P, 2002.

Kirkpatrick, B. J. and Stuart Clarke, eds. *A Bibliography of Virginia Woolf.* 4th ed. New York: Oxford UP, 1998.

Kumar, Shiv. *Bergson and the Stream of Consciousness Novel.* New York: New York UP, 1963.

Lackey, Michael. "Modernist Anti-Philosophicalism and Virginia Woolf's Critique of Philosophy." *Journal of Modern Literature* 29.4 (Summer 2006): 76–98.

Laurence, Patricia. *Lily Briscoe's Chinese Eyes: Bloomsbury, Modernism, and China.* Columbia: U of South Carolina P, 2003.

Lawlor, Leonard and Valentine Moulard. "Henri Bergson." *The Stanford Encyclopedia of Philosophy.* Ed. Edward Zalta. Winter 2008 ed. Web. 10 March 2009. http://plato.stanford.edu/archives/win2008/entries/bergson/.

Leavis, F. R. "After *To the Lighthouse.*" 1941. Vogler 99–100.

Lee, Hermione. *Virginia Woolf.* New York: Vintage, 1996.

Lehmann, John. *Thrown to the Woolfs.* London: Weidenfeld and Nicolson, 1978.

Levenback, Karen. *Virginia Woolf and the Great War.* Syracuse: Syracuse UP, 1998.

Lewis, Wyndham. *Men Without Art.* 1934. Ed. Seamus Cooney. Santa Rosa: Black Sparrow Press, 1987.

Light, Alison. *Mrs. Woolf and the Servants: An Intimate History of Domestic Life in Bloomsbury.* New York: Bloomsbury Press, 2008.

Lilienfeld, Jane. "'The Deceptiveness of Beauty': Mother Love and Mother Hate in *To the Lighthouse.*" *Twentieth Century Literature* 23.3 (Oct. 1977): 345–76.

—. "Where the Spear Plants Grew: The Ramsays' Marriage in *To the Light-house.*" *New Feminist Essays on Virginia Woolf.* Ed. Jane Marcus. Lincoln: U of Nebraska P, 1981. 148–69.

MacCarthy, Desmond. "Bloomsbury: An Unfinished Memoir." 1933. MacCarthy, *Memories* 172–75.

—. *Memories.* London: MacGibbon & Kee, 1953.

—. "Roger Fry and The Post-Impressionist Exhibition of 1910." 1945. MacCarthy, *Memories* 176–85.

MacKay, Marina. "Putting the House in Order: Virginia Woolf and Blitz Modernism." *Modern Language Quarterly* 66.2 (June 2005): 227–52.

Maggio, Paula. "Fun with Virginia on Stage at Fordham." *Blogging Woolf: Focusing on Virginia Woolf and Her Circle, Past and Present.* Created, written, and ed. Paula Maggio. N.p., 14 May 2009. Web. 23 May 2009. http://bloggingwoolf.wordpress.com/page/2/.

Majumdar, Robin and Allen McLaurin, eds. *Virginia Woolf: The Critical Heritage.* New York: Routledge, 1997.

Mansfield, Katherine. *Prelude.* London: Hogarth Press, 1918.

Manson, Janet. "Leonard Woolf as an Architect of the League of Nations." Themed Issue: Virginia Woolf International. *South Carolina Review Online Library* (2007): 1–13.

Marcus, Jane. "Britannia Rules *The Waves.*" Marcus, *Hearts of Darkness* 59–85.

—. *Hearts of Darkness: White Women Write Race.* New Brunswick: Rutgers UP, 2004.

—. "'No More Horses': Virginia Woolf on Art and Propaganda." *Art & Anger: Reading Like a Woman.* Ed. Marcus. Columbus: Ohio State UP, 1988. 101–21.

—. "Taking the Bull by the Udders: Sexual Difference in Virginia Woolf— A Conspiracy Theory." *Virginia Woolf and the Languages of Patriarchy.* By Marcus. Bloomington: Indiana UP, 1987. 136–62.

—. "'A Very Fine Negress.'" Marcus, *Hearts* 24–58.

—, ed. *Virginia Woolf and Bloomsbury: A Centenary Celebration.* Bloomington: Indiana UP, 1987.

Marder, Herbert. *Feminism and Art: A Study of Virginia Woolf.* Chicago: U of Chicago P, 1968.

"Margaret Llewelyn Davies and Emmy Freundlich." Pressure Group Archives: Women of Conviction. University of Hull Archives. Hull, UK. Web. 20 July 2008. http://www.hull.ac.uk/women-of-conviction/women_of_conviction/MLD-and-EF.html#Freundlich.

Markert, Lawrence. Introduction. *The Bloomsbury Group: A Reference Guide.* Boston: G. K. Hall, 1990. x–xv.

Matro, Thomas. "Only Relations: Vision and Achievement in *To the Light-house.*" *PMLA* 99.2 (March 1984): 212–24.

Mayoux, Jean-Jacques. Rev. of *To the Lighthouse*. *Revue Anglo-Americaine* (June 1928): 424–38. Majumdar and McLaurin 214–21.

McKenna, Kathleen. "The Language of Orgasm." Barrett and Cramer, *Re: Reading* 29–38.

McLean, Prince. "In-Depth Review: Kindle 2, the Apple TV of Books." *AppleInsider.com* 4 March 2009. Web. 15 March 2009.

McNichol, Stella, ed. *To the Lighthouse*. By Virginia Woolf. Introd. Hermione Lee. New ed. London: Penguin, 2000.

McVicker, Jeanette. "Postcolonial Approaches." Snaith 209–26.

—. "Reading *To the Lighthouse* as a Critique of the Imperial." Daugherty and Pringle 97–104.

—. "Vast Nests of Chinese Boxes, or Getting from Q to R: Critiquing Empire in 'Kew Gardens' and *To the Lighthouse*." *Virginia Woolf Miscellanies: Proceedings of the First Annual Conference on Virginia Woolf*. Ed. Mark Hussey and Vara Neverow-Turk. New York: Pace UP, 1992. 40–42.

Mellers, W. H. "Virginia Woolf: The Last Phase." *Kenyon Review* 4.3 (Autumn 1942): 381–87.

Mirsky, Dmitri. *The Intelligentsia of Great Britain*. Trans. Alec Brown. London: Victor Gollancz, 1935.

Mitchell, Katie. "Breaking the Waves." *Guardian* 11 Nov. 2006: 14.

Moore, George Edward. *Principia Ethica*. 1903. Cambridge: Cambridge UP, 1959.

Moore, Judy. *The Bloomsbury Trail in Sussex*. Seaford: S. B. Publications, 1995.

Morphet, Richard. "The Art of Vanessa Bell." Introduction. *Vanessa Bell: Paintings and Drawings, 20 November to 12 December 1973*. London: Anthony d'Offay, 1973. 5–13.

Mrs. Dalloway. Screenplay by Eileen Atkins. Dir. Marleen Gorris. Perf. Vanessa Redgrave. First Look International, 1997. Film.

"Mrs. Woolf's New Novel." Rev. of *To the Lighthouse*, by Virginia Woolf. *Times Literary Supplement* 5 May 1927: 315.

Muller, Herbert. "Virginia Woolf, and Feminine Fiction." 1937. Beja, *Critical* 29–37.

Naylor, Gillian, ed. *Bloomsbury: The Artists, Authors and Designers by Themselves*. London: Mitchell Beazley, 1990.

Neverow-Turk, Vara and Mark Hussey, eds. *Virginia Woolf: Themes and Variations: Selected Papers from the Second Annual Conference on Virginia Woolf*. New York: Pace UP, 1993.

Nicolson, Nigel. "Bloomsbury: The Myth and the Reality." Marcus, *Virginia Woolf and Bloomsbury* 7–22.

—. *Portrait of a Marriage*. 1973. Chicago: U of Chicago P, 1998.

Nightingale, Benedict. "Foggy and Missed." *Times* (London). 9 Jan. 1995: 12.

O'Connor, John. "Virginia Woolf's 'To the Lighthouse.'" *New York Times* 12 Oct. 1984: C33.

Olano, Pamela. "'Women Alone Stir My Imagination': Reading Virginia Woolf as a Lesbian." Neverow-Turk and Hussey 158–71.

Oldham, Madeleine. "*To the Lighthouse*: An Introduction." *TheatreForum* 33 (Summer/Fall 2008): 36–38.

Orlando. Dir. and screenplay by Sally Potter. Perf. Tilda Swinton and Quentin Crisp. Adventure Pictures, 1992. Film.

Oxindine, Annette. "Sexing the Epiphany in 'Moments of Being': Woolf's Nice Little Story about Sapphism." *Journal of the Short Story in English* 31 (Autumn 1998): 51–61.

Patmore, Coventry. *The Angel in the House*. 1854. *The Poems of Coventry Patmore*. Ed. Frederick Page. Oxford: Oxford UP, 1949. 61–210

Pedersen, Glenn. "Vision in *To the Lighthouse*." *PMLA* 73.5 (Dec. 1958): 585–600.

Phillips, Kathy. *Virginia Woolf Against Empire*. Knoxville: U of Tennessee P, 1994.

Pratt, Annis. "Sexual Imagery in *To the Lighthouse*: A New Feminist Approach." *Modern Fiction Studies* 18.3 (Autumn 1972): 417–31.

"Press Coverage." Berkeley Repertory Theatre Website. Web. 1 March 2009. http://www.berkeleyrep.org/press/coverage.asp.

Putzel, Steven. "Virginia Woolf and 'The Distance of the Stage.'" *Women's Studies* 28.4 (Sept. 1999): 435–70.

"Q. D. Leavis." Centre for Leavis Studies. University of Surrey. Surrey, UK. Web. 15 July 2008. http://mypages.surrey.ac.uk/eds1cj/qd-leavis-life-and-work.htm.

Raitt, Suzanne. *May Sinclair: A Modern Victorian*. Oxford: Oxford UP, 2000.

—. *Virginia Woolf's* To the Lighthouse. Critical Studies of Key Texts series. New York: Palgrave Macmillan, 1990.

—. *Vita and Virginia: The Work and Friendship of V. Sackville-West and Virginia Woolf*. Oxford: Clarendon Press, 1993.

Ramsden, John, ed. *Oxford Companion to Twentieth-Century British Politics*. Oxford: Oxford UP, 2002.

Reid, Su. *To the Lighthouse*. Critics Debate series. New York: Palgrave Macmillan, 1991.

Reynolds, David. *Britannia Overruled: British Policy and World Power in the Twentieth Century*. New York: Longman, 2000.

Richardson, Dorothy. *Pilgrimage*. 4 vols. 1915–1938. London: Virago, 1979.

Risolo, Donna. "Outing Mrs. Ramsay: Reading the Lesbian Subtext in Virginia Woolf's *To the Lighthouse*." Neverow-Turk and Hussey 238–48.

Roberts, John Hawley. "Toward Virginia Woolf." *Virginia Quarterly Review* 10 (1934): 587–602.

—. "'Vision and Design' in Virginia Woolf." *PMLA* 61.3 (Sept. 1946): 835–47.

Roe, Sue and Susan Sellers, eds. *The Cambridge Companion to Virginia Woolf*. Cambridge: Cambridge UP, 2000.

A Room of One's Own. Adapt. and dir. Patrick Garland. Perf. Eileen Atkins. Hampstead Theatre, London. 1989. Performance.

Rosenbaum, S. P. *Aspects of Bloomsbury: Studies in Modern English Literary and Intellectual History*. New York: St. Martin's Press, 1998.

—, ed. *The Bloomsbury Group: A Collection of Memoirs, Commentary and Criticism*. London: Croom Helm, 1975.

—, ed. *A Bloomsbury Group Reader*. Oxford: Blackwell, 1993.

—. *Edwardian Bloomsbury: The Early Literary History of the Bloomsbury Group*. New York: Palgrave Macmillan, 1994.

—. *Georgian Bloomsbury: The Early Literary History of the Bloomsbury Group*. New York: Palgrave Macmillan, 2004.

—. Introduction. Rosenbaum, *Collection* 1–3.

—. "Leonard Woolf: The Beginnings of The Hogarth Press." Rosenbaum, *Collection* 117–18.

—. "Roger Fry: A Great Historical Portrait Group of Bloomsbury." Rosenbaum, *Collection* 19.

—. *Victorian Bloomsbury: The Early Literary History of the Bloomsbury Group*. New York: St. Martin's, 1987.

—."Virginia Woolf and the Intellectual Origins of Bloomsbury." *Virginia Woolf: Centennial Essays*. Ed. Elaine Ginsberg and Laura Moss Gottlieb. Troy: The Whiston Publishing Company, 1983. 11–26.

Rosenberg, Beth Carole and Jeanne Dubino, eds. *Virginia Woolf and the Essay*. New York: St. Martin's, 1997.

Russell, Bertrand. *The Analysis of Matter*. 1927. 3rd ed. London: Routledge, 1992.

—. *The Selected Letters of Bertrand Russell*. Ed. Nicholas Griffin. Vol. 1. Boston: Houghton Mifflin, 1992.

Russell, H. K. "Woolf's *To the Lighthouse*." *Explicator* 8 (Nov. 1949): Q2.

Sackville-West, Vita. *The Letters of Vita Sackville-West to Virginia Woolf*. Ed. Louise DeSalvo and Mitchell Leaska. New York: William Morrow, 1985.

Sarker, Sonita. "Modernisms in Our Image . . . Always, Partially." *Modernism/modernity* 13.3 (2006): 561–66.

Schroder, Leena Kore. "Tales of Abjection and Miscegenation: Virginia Woolf's and Leonard Woolf's 'Jewish' Stories." *Twentieth Century Literature* 49.3 (Autumn 2003): 298–327.

Scott, Bonnie Kime, ed. *The Gender of Modernism: A Critical Anthology*. Bloomington: Indiana UP, 1990.

Scott, Sir Walter. *The Antiquary*. 1816. "Magnum Opus" ed. 1929. Oxford: Oxford UP, 2002.

Second Life: Woolf World. Created by Elisa Kay Sparks and Clemson University students. N.p. Web. 8 June 2009. http://21woolfworld.blogspot.com/.

Seshagiri, Urmila. "Orienting Virginia Woolf: Race, Aesthetics, and Politics in *To the Lighthouse*." *Modern Fiction Studies* 50.1 (Spring 2004): 58–84.

Shakespeare, William. "Sonnet 98." 1609. *Virginia Woolf Web*. Archive, 1995–99. Web. 15 Nov. 2008. http://orlando.jp.org/VWWARC/DAT/sonnet98.html.

Shank, Adele Edling, adapt. *To the Lighthouse*. *TheatreForum* 33 (Summer/Fall 2008): 40–65.

Shaw, John. "'Luriana, Lurilee' Revisited I: 'A Garden Song': Leonard Woolf's Manuscript Copy: The 'Right Version' of the Poem?" *Notes and Queries* 52.1 (March 2005): 89–93.

Shelley, Percy B. "To Jane: The Invitation." 1822. *Poetry Foundation*. Web. 15 Nov. 2008. http://www.poetryfoundation.org/archive/poem.html?id=180603.

Sherman, David. "A Plot Unraveling into Ethics: Woolf, Levinas, and 'Time Passes.'" *Woolf Studies Annual* 13 (2007): 159–79.

Shone, Richard. *Bloomsbury Portraits: Vanessa Bell, Duncan Grant, and Their Circle*. Oxford: Phaidon, 1976.

Silver, Brenda. "Textual Criticism as Feminist Practice: Or, Who's Afraid of Virginia Woolf Part II." *Representing Modernist Texts: Editing as Interpretation*. Ed. George Bornstein. Ann Arbor: U of Michigan P, 1991. 193–222.

—. *Virginia Woolf Icon*. Chicago: U of Chicago P, 1999.

Sinclair, May. "The Novels of Dorothy Richardson." *Egoist* 5 (April 1918): 57–59.

Snaith, Anna, ed. *Palgrave Advances in Virginia Woolf Studies*. New York: Palgrave Macmillan, 2007.

Spalding, Frances. *Vanessa Bell*. New Haven: Ticknor & Fields, 1983.

Sparks, Elisa Kay. *Vision Statement*. 1996. Computer-generated design for silk screen. Private collection. Web. 27 Nov. 2008. http:// hubcap.clemson. edu/~sparks/visionwg.htm.

Spivak, Gayatri. "Unmaking and Making in *To the Lighthouse*." *In Other Worlds: Essays in Cultural Politics*. By Spivak. New York: Routledge, 1988. 30–45.

Stalla, Heidi. "William Bankes: Echoes of Egypt in Virginia Woolf's *To the Lighthouse*." *Woolf Studies Annual* 14 (2008): 21–34.

Steinberg, Erwin. "Freudian Symbolism and Communication." *Literature and Psychology* 3 (April 1953): 2–5.

Stephen, Julia. *Julia Duckworth Stephen: Stories for Children, Essays for Adults*. Ed. Diane Filby Gillespie and Elizabeth Steele. Syracuse: Syracuse UP, 1993.

—. *Notes from Sick Rooms*. 1883. Whitefish, MT: Kessinger, 2008.

Stephen, Leslie, ed. *Dictionary of National Biography*. London: Smith Elder, & Co., 1885–1891. 26 vols.

—. *Mausoleum Book*. Ed. Alan Bell. Oxford: Oxford UP, 1977.

Stewart, Jack. "Color in *To the Lighthouse*." *Twentieth Century Literature* 31.4 (Winter 1985): 438–58.

Stockton, Sharon. "Public Space and Private Time: Perspective in *To the Lighthouse* and in Einstein's Special Theory." *Essays in Arts and Sciences* 27 (Oct. 1998): 95–115.

Swanson, Diana. "The Lesbian Feminism of Woolf's *To the Lighthouse*." Barrett and Cramer, *Re: Reading* 38–44.

Swinnerton, Frank. *The Georgian Scene: A Literary Panorama*. New York: Farrar & Rinehart, 1934.

—. Review. *Observer* 20 July 1941: 3. Majumdar and Allen 442.

Taylor, Nicole Estvanik. "Songs of Innovation and Experience." *American Theatre* 26.2 (Feb. 2009): 34–41.

Tennyson, Alfred Lord. "The Charge of the Light Brigade." 1854. *Poetry Foundation*. Web. 15 Nov. 2008. http://www.poetryfoundation.org.

Tickner, Lisa. "*Studland Beach*, Domesticity, and 'Significant Form.'" *Representations* 65 Special issue: New Perspectives in British Studies (Winter 1999): 63–92.

To the Lighthouse. Adapt. Lindsay Bell. Dir. Ann Hodges. Shaw Festival Theatre, Niagara-on-the-Lake, Canada. 3 August 2000. Radio performance.

To the Lighthouse. Adapt. Julia Limer. Dir. Andrew Holmes. Empty Space Theatre Company, London. 4 Jan. to 28 Jan. 1995. Performance.

To the Lighthouse. Adapt. Adele Edling Shank. Dir. Les Waters. Music by Paul Dresher. Berkeley Repertory Theatre, Berkeley, CA. 23 Feb. to 25 March 2007. Performance.

To the Lighthouse. Adapt. Hugh Stoddart. Dir. Colin Gregg. Perf. Rosemary Harris and Kenneth Branagh. BBC Television, 1983. Film.

Troy, William. "Virginia Woolf and the Novel of Sensibility." 1932. Beja, *Casebook* 85–89.

Usui, Masami. "Lily as One of the Women Painters of the St. Ives School." *Virginia Woolf Bulletin of the Virginia Woolf Society of Great Britain* 4 (May 2000): 13–16.

Vanita, Ruth. "Bringing Buried Things to Light: Homoerotic Alliances in *To the Lighthouse*." Barrett and Cramer, *Virginia Woolf: Lesbian* 165–79.

Veltman, Chloe. "Les Waters: Explorer with an Ear." *American Theatre* (Dec. 2007): 42–47.

—. "A Stage of One's Own." *San Francisco Weekly* 14 Match 2007. Web. 23 Nov. 2008.

Vogler, Thomas, ed. *Twentieth Century Interpretations of* To the Lighthouse*: A Collection of Critical Essays*. Englewood Cliffs: Prentice-Hall, 1970.

Waves. Dir. and devised by Katie Mitchell. Video designed by Leo Warner for Fifty-Nine Ltd. National Theatre of Great Britain, London. 9 Nov. 2006 to 8 Feb. 2007. Performance.

Weil, Lise. "Entering a Lesbian Field of Vision: *To the Lighthouse* and *Between the Acts*." Barrett and Cramer, *Virginia Woolf: Lesbian* 241–58.

Whitworth, Michael. *Virginia Woolf*. Authors in Context series. Oxford: Oxford UP, 2005.

Wildstrom, Stephen. "Amazon's Kindle 2: Delight Is in the Details." *BusinessWeek.com* 24 Feb. 2009. Web. 15 March 2009.

Wilson, Deborah. "Fishing for Woolf's Submerged Lesbian Text." Barrett and Cramer, *Re: Reading* 121–28.

Wilson, Jean Moorcroft. *Virginia Woolf and Anti-Semitism*. Bloomsbury Heritage Series. London: Cecil Woolf, 1995.

Winston, Janet. "'Something Out of Harmony': *To the Lighthouse* and the Subject(s) of Empire." *Woolf Studies Annual* 2 (1996): 39–70.

Winterson, Jeanette. *Art Objects: Essays on Ecstasy and Effrontery*. London: Vintage, 1997.

—. *Lighthousekeeping*. New York: Harcourt, 2006.

—. "Virginia Woolf: Monk's House, Rodmell, E. Sussex." *Writers and Their Houses: A Guide to the Writers' Houses of England, Scotland, Wales and Ireland*. Ed. Kate Marsh. London: Hamish Hamilton, 1993. 460–68.

Woolf, Leonard. *Beginning Again: An Autobiography of the Years 1911 to 1918*. New York: Harcourt, 1964.

—. *Downhill All the Way: An Autobiography of the Years 1919 to 1939*. London: Hogarth Press, 1967.

—. *International Government*. New York: Brentano's, 1916.

—. *Sowing: An Autobiography of the Years 1880 to 1904*. New York: Harcourt, 1960.

Woolf, Virginia. "The Common Reader." 1925. V. Woolf, *Essays* 4 19.

—. *The Diary of Virginia Woolf*. Ed. Anne Olivier Bell. 5 Vols. New York: Harcourt, 1977–79.

—. *The Essays of Virginia Woolf*. Ed. Stuart Clarke. Vol. 5. 5 vols. to date. London: Chatto & Windus, 2009.

—. *The Essays of Virginia Woolf*. Ed. Andrew McNeillie. Vols. 1–4. 5 vols. to date. New York: Harcourt, 1986–1994.

—. *Flush: A Biography*. New York: Mariner, 1976.

—. Foreword to *Catalogue of Recent Paintings by Vanessa Bell*. London: Lefevre Galleries, 1934.

—. "How Should One Read a Book?" Sept. 1925. Holograph fragment of 1926 lecture. V. Woolf, To the Lighthouse: *The Original Holograph Draft* 55–56. MS. The Henry W. and Albert A. Berg Collection of English and American Literature, The New York Public Library, New York.

—. "How Should One Read a Book?" Nov. 1925. Holograph draft of 1926 lecture. Daugherty, "Virginia Woolf's" 137–85. MS. The Henry W. and Albert A. Berg Collection of English and American Literature, The New York Public Library, New York.

—. "How Should One Read a Book?" 1926. V. Woolf, *Essays* 4 388–400.

—. "How Should One Read a Book?" 1932. V. Woolf, *Essays* 5 572–84.

—. *The Letters of Virginia Woolf*. Ed. Nigel Nicolson and Joanne Trautmann. 6 vols. New York: Harcourt, 1975–1980.

—. "Literary Geography." 1905. V. Woolf, *Essays* 1 32–36.

—. "The Love of Reading." 1931. V. Woolf, *Essays* 5 271–75.

—. "Modern Fiction." 1925. V. Woolf, *Essays* 4 157-65.

—. "Modern Novels (Joyce)." B. Scott 642–45. MS. The Henry W. and Albert A. Berg Collection of English and American Literature, The New York Public Library, New York.

—. "Moments of Being: 'Slater's Pins Have No Points.'" *The Complete Shorter Fiction of Virginia Woolf*. Ed. Susan Dick. 2nd ed. New York: Harvest, 1989. 215-20.

—. "Mr. Bennett and Mrs. Brown." 1923. V. Woolf, *Essays* 3 384-89.

—. *Mrs. Dalloway*. 1925. New York: Harcourt, 1953.

—. "Notes on an Elizabethan Play." 1925. V. Woolf, *Essays* 4 62–70.

—. *Orlando*. London: Hogarth Press, 1928.

—. *A Passionate Apprentice: The Early Journals 1897–1909*. Ed. Mitchell Leaska. New York: Harcourt, 1990.

—. *Recent Paintings by Vanessa Bell*. London: The London Artists' Association, 1930.

—. "Romance and the Heart." Rev. of *Revolving Lights*, by Dorothy Richardson. 1923. Woolf, *Essays* 3 365–68.

—. *A Room of One's Own*. 1929. New York: Harcourt, 1981.

—. *The Second Common Reader*. New York: Harvest, 1960.

—. "A Sketch of the Past." 1940. *Moments of Being*. 2nd ed. Ed. Jeanne Schulkind. New York: Harcourt, 1985. 64–159.

—. "Le temps passe" ["Time Passes"]. Trans. Charles Mauron. *Commerce: Cahiers Trimestriels Publiés par les Soins de Paul Valéry, Léon-Paul Fargue, Valery Larbaud* 10 (Winter 1926): 89–133.

—. *Three Guineas*. London: Hogarth Press, 1938.

—. *To the Lighthouse*. 1927. New York: Harcourt, 1981.

—. *To the Lighthouse*. Kindle ed. Oakgrove, 2008. Digital file.

—. *To the Lighthouse*. Introd. Eavan Boland and Maud Ellmann. New ed. London: Vintage, 2004.

—. *To the Lighthouse*. Narr. Phyllida Law. Unabridged ed. BBC Audiobooks, 2004. CD.

—. *To the Lighthouse*. Narr. Juliet Stevenson. Unabridged ed. Naxos Audio-Books, 2008. CD.

—. To the Lighthouse*: The Original Holograph Draft*. Ed. Susan Dick. Toronto: U of Toronto P, 1982. MS. The Henry W. and Albert A. Berg Collection of English and American Literature, The New York Public Library, New York.

—. *The Virginia Woolf Manuscripts: From The Henry W. and Albert A. Berg Collection at The New York Public Library*. Microfilm. Woodbridge: Research Publications International, 1993.

—. *The Virginia Woolf Reader*. Ed. Mitchell Leaska. New York: Harcourt, 1984.

—. *The Waves*. London: Hogarth Press, 1931.

—. *The Years*. London: Hogarth Press, 1937.

Woolf, Virginia and Vanessa Bell with Thoby Stephen. *Hyde Park Gate News: The Stephen Family Newspaper*. Ed. Gill Lowe. London: Hesperus Press, 2005.

Woolf Online: An Electronic Edition and Commentary of Virginia Woolf's "Time Passes." Created by Julia Briggs, Peter Shillingsburg, and Marilyn Deegan. www.woolfonline.com.

Working Group on Jews, Media and Religion. "The Dreyfus Affair through Postcards." *MODIYA Project: Jews/Media/Religion*. Center for Religion and Media. New York University. N.d. Web. 6 June 2008. http://modiya. nyu.edu/modiya/handle/1964/375.

Zola, Émile. "J'accuse . . . !: Lettre au Président de la République" ["I Accuse . . . !: Open Letter to the President of the French Republic"]. *L'Aurore* 13 Jan. 1898. "'J'accuse . . . !' Émile Zola, L'Aurore and the Dreyfus Affair." "The Dreyfus Affair and Anti-Semitism." *Virtual Absinthe Museum*. Oxygénée, Ltd. N.d. Web. 6 June 2008. http://www.oxygenee.com/Zola-and-Dreyfus. pdf.

Zwerdling, Alex. *Virginia Woolf and the Real World*. Berkeley: U of California P, 1986.

INDEX